The Abingdon
African American Preaching Library
Volume I

The Abingdon African American Preaching Library

Volume 1

KIRK BYRON JONES

EDITOR

Abingdon Press
Nashville

THE ABINGDON AFRICAN AMERICAN PREACHING LIBRARY: VOLUME I

This book is printed on acid-free paper.

Library of Congress Cataloging-in-Publication Data

The Abingdon African American preaching library / Kirk Byron Jones, editor.
   p. cm.
Includes index.
ISBN 0-687-33305-9 (binding: printed casebound: alk. paper)
   1. African American preaching. 2. Bible—Sermons—Outlines, syllabi, etc. 3. Church year sermons—Outlines, syllabi, etc. I. Jones, Kirk Byron. II. Abingdon Press. III. Title: African American preaching library.

BV4221.A35   2006
251.0089'96073—dc22

                             2006013166

06 07 08 09 10 11 12 13 14 15—10 9 8 7 6 5 4 3 2 1

MANUFACTURED IN THE UNITED STATES OF AMERICA

To all called and committed to the
faithful play of preaching.

CONTENTS

FEBRUARY——AFRICAN AMERICAN HERITAGE MONTH

Article

Sermon Outlines

MARCH

Article

Sermon Outlines

Contents

APRIL

MAY

Article

Contents

Sermon Outlines

JUNE

Articles

Contents

July

AUGUST

Article

Sermon Outlines

September

Contents

OCTOBER

Article

Sermon Outlines

November

Article

Sermon Outlines

Contents

December

Articles

Sermon Outlines

Contents

INTRODUCTION

In Episode 1 of the classic video documentary *Eyes on the Prize: America's Civil Rights Years*, Rufus Lewis attempts to explain the preaching effect of the Montgomery Improvement Association's dynamic new leader, Martin Luther King Jr. Lewis's demeanor is like a child explaining a marvelous birthday experience. He smiles and laughs and rocks back and forth in his chair, expressing with his face and gesturing with his hands sentiments that are, for the most part, beyond words. Lewis does manage to say King's speaking was a "moving, stimulating thing" that "went right through you." He marvels how King would be "taken away" by his own speech.

Ask anyone reared in the African American church tradition to describe the power of black preaching and you will probably get a response similar to the one offered by Rufus Lewis. How do you explain something that has the power to create—in a moment—joy, hope, and life time and time again? Enthusiastically, lovingly, and, ultimately, incompletely.

Two features come to mind regarding the source of black preaching's unique and wonderful power. First, black preaching is rooted in life. Like the parabolic preaching of its central spiritual character, Jesus, black preaching takes its cues from the everyday ebb and flow of black existence. Illustrations, topics, points, and ideas are never far from the highways and side streets of daily living. Thus, black preaching, at its best, is connected. Even if you are not a frequent churchgoer, you should be able to understand the preacher because he or she is speaking to you about you and your life. So, in the words of the famous gospel lyric, when it comes to listening to black preaching, "You don't need no ticket . . . you just get on board."

Second, preaching in the African American heritage is *feeling-full*. Black preachers preach to the heart and head because black congregants would and will have it no other way. There is a familiar expression in the tradition: "I wouldn't have a religion I couldn't feel sometime." The expression is an understatement. Most black church folk I know will not have a religion they cannot feel *most* of the time. Thoughts are not better or higher than feelings; thoughts and feelings go hand in hand. Thus, the preacher had better feel his sermon and do his best to make others feel it. From the beginning, "Preach to all of me" has been the unspoken, quintessential request of black churchgoers. Skilled black preachers deduced early on that holistic preaching required rigorous thoughtfulness, free emotion, expansive imagining, and an abiding spiritual undergirding. Such attributes survive, not mainly because black preachers call them forth, but because black congregants will not allow for anything less.

Now, concerning the book you are holding. *The Abingdon African American Preaching Library* seeks to help preachers of all traditions cultivate a creative and spirited preaching consciousness. Here are seven primary presumptions about preaching—not just black preaching—loitering in the editor's mind:

1. Though laced with gravity and seriousness, preaching is essentially a joyous affair.
2. There are a thousand and more ways to conceptualize, organize, and preach any sermon.
3. Life, as well as book learning, provides endless streams of preaching content.
4. Moving preaching comes through preachers who, themselves, are moved by words and by Word and, just as much, by living.
5. Words are but half of preaching; pauses and the unstated are the other half.

6. Noticing precedes saying. Take time to pay attention to all
   of it and you will have more than enough to say.
7. Stillness of mind is the secret to preaching that matters
   most.

Use this book of outlines to stimulate your own feeling, imagining, and thinking. Resist lifting ideas word for word. Route
what you read through the lanes of your own experience and critical thinking. Mess with the outlines in this book. Write, scrib-
ble, draw, and doodle in this book. Play with the outlines, the
long ones, the short ones, the scholarly ones, the earthy ones, the
ones that inspire you, and the ones that leave you feeling that you
can do much better. Go ahead and do a better outline. We dare
you! Turn the outlines around and over; delete, add, or even
ignore some completely after they have done the job of inspiring
you to go off in a totally different direction. Most of all, have
faithful fun with this *workbook* and future volumes to the end of
consistently enlivened sermon preparation and preaching.

My deepest gratitude to Abingdon Press for inspiring this
project. Deep gratitude to the accomplished, esteemed, and
skilled contributors to this first volume in *The Abingdon African
American Preaching Library*: Gilbert H. Caldwell, Teresa Fry
Brown, Cheryl Kirk-Duggan, Portia Wills Lee, Cedric Kirkland-
Harris, Marsha Brown Woodard, Charles Henry, and Jeffrey
Brown. Elsewhere in this volume, you will find their biographical
and contact information. If their sermons inspire you, don't hes-
itate to drop them a line of appreciation.

Finally, engage and enjoy this initial installment in *The African
American Preaching Library*.

Kirk Byron Jones, Editor
November 2005

January

ARTICLES

Remembering the Whole Martin Luther King Jr.

Kirk Byron Jones

I n *Martin Luther King: The Inconvenient Hero*, historian Vincent Harding, a former friend of Dr. King, fears that we are experiencing "a national amnesia" regarding King. Harding writes:

> Somehow it appears that we are determined to hold this hero captive to the powerful period in his life that culminated in the magnificent March on Washington of 1963, refusing to allow him to break out of the stunning eloquence of "I Have a Dream." My hope is that we might press ourselves beyond amnesia to engage the tougher and more difficult King. ([Maryknoll, N.Y.: Orbis Books, 1996], vii)

What does Harding mean by "the tougher and more difficult King" of post-1963? Could the pre-1963 Martin King have been any tougher? In 1955, at the age of twenty-six, just a year after becoming pastor of the Dexter Avenue Baptist Church in Montgomery and less than a year after receiving his Ph.D. degree from Boston University, Martin King was elected president of the Montgomery Improvement Association. He assumed leadership of a 381-day bus boycott ignited by Rosa Parks and participated in by thousands of people. In 1956, his home—where he lived with his bride of three years, Coretta, and their two-month-old daughter, Yolanda—was bombed.

In 1957, the still new husband, father, pastor, and community leader became founding president of the Southern Christian Leadership Conference.

In 1958, King was arrested in Montgomery and was stabbed almost to death in Harlem. During surgery, the sharp blade of the letter opener had been found dangerously close to King's aorta. Had King merely sneezed, he would have died.

Between 1960 and 1963, Martin Luther King was arrested in Atlanta, Albany, and Birmingham. Birmingham is where King penned his legendary "Letter from Birmingham Jail," a letter that was written in response to fellow white clergy who had accused King of being "a disturber of the peace" and an "outside agitator," a troublemaker. Birmingham is also the place where King's headquarters, his brother's home, and the Sixteenth Avenue Baptist Church were bombed. The latter tragedy killed four girls attending Sunday school: Carole Robertson, Cynthia Wesley, Denise McNair, and Addie Mae Collins. With a broken and heavy heart, Martin King preached at a joint funeral service for the victims. He said later that it was the first time he saw his dream turn into a nightmare. The pre-1963 King was tough enough. He dreamed, dared to deploy the dream, and weathered the brutal social, physical, and emotional storm that followed.

With King's battle scars and wounds in full view, what is Vincent Harding's point when he urges us to press beyond amnesia to engage a "tougher" Martin Luther King Jr.?

After 1963, Martin King began to say and write words that were tougher and more difficult for many in America to accept, including some of his most ardent admirers. If his words were tougher for his contemporaries to hear and accept, then they are perhaps even more difficult for many to accept now. Yet, a more responsible celebration of Martin Luther King Jr.'s birthday will not deny entrance to such words. Listen to some of King's words from his final book, *The Trumpet of Conscience*, with this question in mind: Can we afford not to remember them?

> A true revolution of values will soon cause us to question the fairness and justice of many of our past and present policies. A true revolution of values will soon look uneasily on the glaring contrast between poverty and wealth. (p.32)
>
> The developed industrial nations of the world cannot remain secure islands of prosperity in a seething sea of poverty. The storm is rising against the privileged minority of the earth, from which there is no shelter in isolation and armament. The storm will not abate until a just distribution of the fruits of the

earth enables [people] everywhere to live in dignity and human decency. (p.17)

Our world is sick with war. . . . There may have been a time when war served as a negative good by preventing the spread and growth of an evil force, but the very destructive power of modern weapons of warfare eliminates even the possibility that war may any longer serve as a negative good. (pp. 67-68)

We must find new ways to speak for peace. . . . If we do not act, we shall surely be dragged down the long, dark, and shameful corridors of time reserved for those who possess power without compassion, might without morality, and strength without sight. ([New York: Harper & Row, 1968], 33-34)

In choosing to leave out the more controversial elements of King's sociopolitical prophecy, we risk living out the poetic lament of Carl Wendell Himes Jr.'s poem "Now That He Is Safely Dead":

Let us praise him . . .
Dead men make
    such convenient heroes.

Practicing Margin in Ministry

Kirk Byron Jones

A book that has had a positive, lasting influence on my life is entitled *Margin: Restoring Emotional, Physical, Financial, and Time Reserves to Overloaded Lives* by Richard A. Swenson (Colorado Springs, Colo.: NavPress, 1992). Dr. Swenson's socially relevant and spiritually valid thesis is that we must allow more time and space between ourselves and our limits if we are to be well and whole. Clear and incontestable is his argument that overloaded living is both unhealthy and unholy:

> We are not infinite. The day does not have more than twenty-four hours. We do not have an inexhaustible source of human energy. We cannot keep running on empty. Limits are real, and despite what some stoics might think, limits are not even an enemy. Overloading is the enemy.
>
> Some will respond: "I can do all things through Christ who strengthens me." Can you? Can you fly? Can you go six months without eating? Neither can you live a healthy life chronically overloaded. God did not intend this verse to represent a negation of life balance. Jesus did not heal all. He did not minister to all. He did not visit all. He did not teach all. He did not work twenty-hour ministry days.
>
> It is God the Creator who made limits, and it is the same God who placed them within us for our protection. We exceed them at our peril (p. 77).

I believe there are steps that we, as preachers, can and must take in order to observe a calmer and more peaceful pace in ministry. First, we can develop a ministry schedule that, ideally, limits our workweek to a range of forty-five to fifty-five hours and that allows for sufficient time (Swenson's *margin*) for solitude, rest, play, and quality time with our family and friends. (I wonder how much immorality in ministry is directly linked to improper self-care.) Second, we can monitor our schedules so that we do not overbook preaching, teaching, and speaking engagements. For many of us the hardest, yet perhaps the most important, challenge we face is learning to say no. Third, we can learn more deeply just what it is to live within the grace and love of God that we preach and teach and to, in the process, lose our addictions to adrenaline, achievement, and acceptance: three honorable but potentially lethal sources of much of our striving.

As we come upon that moment in which we celebrate with greater emphasis the gift of God who is the Prince of Peace, let us move toward observing more peace—*margin*—in our living and ministry. It may very well be the best gift you can give to yourself, your family, and those to whom you minister.

JANUARY

SERMON OUTLINES

Week One

Sing a New Song!

Marsha Brown Woodward

Text

Isaiah 42:9-10

Theme

To remember that each generation needs its own song from God.

Sermon Outline

WE NEED A NEW SONG

Howard Thurman wrote:

> The old song of my spirit has wearied itself out. It has long ago been learned by heart so that now it repeats itself over and over, bringing no added joy to my days or lift to my spirit. . . .
>
> I will sing a new song. . . . I must learn the new song that is capable of meeting the new need. I must fashion new words born of all the new growth of my life, my mind and my spirit. I must prepare for new melodies that have never been mine before, that all that is within me may lift my voice unto God. . . .
>
> Thus, I may rejoice with each new day and delight my spirit in each fresh unfolding. I will sing this day, a new song unto Thee, O God. (From *Meditations of the Heart* by Howard Thurman [Boston: Beacon Press, 1953], 206)

What are you still doing that has never worked, but because you have gotten into a habit of doing, you continue to do it? What is the new thing that God is doing or speaking in your life?

ISAIAH SPEAKS OF THE NEED OF A NEW SONG

Israel was in exile and was discouraged, and yet the prophet perceived that the season after exile would call for a different mind-set. The challenge is to start thinking in a new way before the new has come. God is an announcer, proclaiming a new order and understanding.

FREEDOM IS NOT ALWAYS FREE
An Exile Called Slavery

In the United States during the time of slavery, there were men and women who heard a new song and began to dream dreams of freedom. Harriet Tubman and Frederick Douglass presented two different approaches to hearing and singing a new song.

An Exile Called Jim Crow Laws

In the early years of the twentieth century, though freedom had come, laws were established to maintain segregation. James Weldon Johnson took the old song of slavery to create a new song for the then-current generation in the writing of "Lift Every Voice and Sing." The song describes the past and the way that the previous generations had sought to be faithful. But the song also asks the current generation to face the challenges of this age.

An Exile Called This Age

Although not in physical slavery, we may still be in bondage today to habits, attitudes, addictions, schedules, and work. Help the congregation think about what controls them and where their priorities might be to make the connection to a more subtle form of slavery.

IT HAS BEEN ANNOUNCED AND DECLARED THAT A NEW SONG IS POSSIBLE

The good news of the text is that in spite of our seeming resistance to live free even when we are, God continually declares freedom and a new season and song.

Considerations and Resources

• Consider the ways that people in the congregation define freedom. It may be fun to take a quick poll during some meetings in the weeks preceding the sermon.

• How have people experienced exile? Are there illustrations from the community or congregation that will give life to the meaning of exile in our time? Consider feeling words that will paint a word picture of the emotion of exile.

• For this sermon, consider singing "Lift Every Voice and Sing" earlier in the service to help the congregation hear the words again. A phrase from each verse could be used during the sermon.

• If you include a moment with children during your worship, continue the concept of new song by asking them to think of new songs they have learned (be careful, some new lyrics learned by youth are shocking) or even by teaching them a new song.

• While suggested for African American Heritage Month, this sermon may be preached at any time during the church year.

My Thoughts and Ideas

_____

_____

_____

_____

Let There Be Laughter!

Text

Genesis 18:9-15

Theme

To explore and celebrate the spiritual power of humor.

Sermon Outline

OWNING OUR LAUGHTER

What and who made you laugh as a child? What and who makes you laugh now?

I remember seeing "Moms" Mabley (Loretta Mary Aiken) on the *Ed Sullivan Show* when I was a child. I think I laughed at first because my father laughed. But then this older black woman dressed in funny clothes, with a funny looking hat, made funny faces, and said funny things that made me laugh. Making children laugh is high and holy work. As my seventeen-year-old son laughed with me during a movie featuring "Moms" Mabley, I marveled at Moms' magical generational range. At one point, I leaned back and told Jared, "She was a kind of priest who made hurting people laugh in the middle of some-times brutal truth, and through their laughter they were able to keep on living."

SARAH LAUGHS

Sarah laughs because she overhears a surprise dinner guest say something really, really funny. He assures ninety-year-old Sarah and one-hundred-year-old Abraham that they are going to be the proud parents of a bouncing baby boy. "A baby!" Sarah shakes her head and laughs to herself.

And she thinks: "I can see it now, me at my age, pushing a baby stroller up main street. A baby at ninety. I can just hear myself calling out to Abraham, 'Abe, while you're out, don't forget to pick up some diapers!'" This guy, whoever he is, has had a little too much grape juice.

Maybe he has, but Sarah soon discovers, whatever the stranger's emotional state, he can still hear pretty well. He has heard Sarah's private (and not-so-private) laughter and calls her on it. She, perhaps embarrassed at getting caught, denies that she laughed.

In my imagined version of how it went, Sarah and the stranger go back and forth like children on a playground: "You laughed," says the stranger. "Did not," Sarah responds. "Did too." "Did not." Just when it appears that Sarah will have the last word, as the stranger walks off into the distance but before he is completely out of sight, he suddenly turns and yells, "Did to!" The stranger is set on Sarah owning her laughter.

WATCH FOR ENEMIES OF DELIGHT

• Alan Jones has written a marvelous book, *Sacrifice and Delight: Spirituality for Ministry*. He writes:

> We have to be on the watch for enemies of delight. . . . In some ways, the organization of the church looks as if it has arranged things precisely to see to it that the Spirit is kept in check, to see that nothing happens, least of all the breaking of delight. Deadliness has a terrible mystery about it because it is not really dead. It is depressingly alive, the active enemy of delight. ([San Francisco: HarperSanFrancisco, 1992], 150)

• As the church can be an enemy of delight, social oppression is such an enemy. In the amazing book *The Color Purple*, a broken Sophia laments, "I know what it feels like to want to sing, and have it beat out you" (New York: Harcourt Brace Jovanovich, 1982).

• Fear, doubt, and cynicism are enemies of delight. How dare we laugh freely and frequently when there is so much wrong about and around us?

DARE TO LAUGH

How dare we *not laugh* freely and frequently when there is so much wrong about and around us? In *Martin & Malcolm & America: A Dream or a Nightmare*, James Cone notes the role of laughter in the lives of Martin King and Malcolm X, and the continuing power of laughter for activism today:

> To fight for life is to experience the joy of life. To laugh, to have fun, is to bear witness to life against death. Freedom-fighters are fun-loving people. Therefore let us laugh, let us shout for joy, not as an indication that we are no longer angry but rather as a sign that we have just begun to fight. ([Maryknoll, N.Y. Orbis Books, 1991], 309)

Laughter is a mysterious energizer. Sometimes when I laugh myself dizzy, it is almost as if I am momentarily lifted out of life. Yet, deep laughter brings us to life and brings life to us in new and invigorating ways.

THE LAST LAUGH

"You laughed, Sarah," the mysterious stranger with divine fingerprints says, not once condemning her for it. They all have the last laugh because the stranger's prophecy comes to pass. Sarah and Abraham bring Isaac—which in Hebrew means "he laughs"—into the world. Sarah got the joke, something Alice Walker calls "the true wine of astonishment. We are not over when we think we are" (from the poem "My Friend Yeshi" in *Absolute Trust in the Goodness of the Earth* [New York: Random House, 2003], 142-45).

Considerations and Resources

• Read or review some of the books identified in the sermon outline.

• Talk to a physician about the physical attributes associated with laughter.

• Review the role of laughter in your life.

• Rediscover the things that made you laugh as a child.

• Identify other humorous episodes in Scripture.

My Thoughts and Ideas

_____

_____

_____

_____

_____

Week Two

Drum Majors for Justice

Cheryl Kirk-Duggan

Text

Amos 5:21-24

Theme

We are called to justice, called away from living in an unhealthy society, and are so sick that our survival is in jeopardy.

Sermon Outline

AMOS AND JUSTICE

Amos is a classical prophet of the eighth century. This prophet for northern Israel preached a message of doom; called for repentance; and spoke against relying on military strength, immorality, social injustice, and meaningless piety. The theme in Amos is a protest against social injustices in Northern Israel during King Jeroboam's reign. YHWH punishes the violation of injustice, allows foreign power to capture them, and ends Israel's national existence. The general point for the text is that the problem is the nature not of worship, but of the worshipers. God does not accept the worship of those who are not interested in justice in their daily lives.

MARTIN LUTHER KING JR., A MODERN AMOS, CALLS US TO BE DRUM MAJORS FOR JUSTICE

- King preached his sermon "The Drum Major Instinct" on February 6, 1968, at Ebenezer Baptist Church two months before he was assassinated.
- The drum major instinct is the desire to be in front, to lead the parade, to be first. We all have the drum major instinct, a tool for good or ill.
- Positively, we can become drum majors for justice, leaders of caring for others, ecologically sensitive, and aware of how we participate daily in oppression.

THE DRUM MAJOR INSTINCT DOES NOT SHIELD US FROM FEAR, PAIN, AND DOUBT

In his book *Stride toward Freedom* (New York: Harper & Row, 1958), King recounts his midnight experience of questioning. When helping lead the Montgomery Bus Boycott, King confronted a personal faith crisis. The boycott ran from Monday, December 5, 1955, through November 5 1956, when the U.S. Supreme Court declared that segregation on public buses was unconstitutional.

King's parents provided love and all his needs; he sailed through college, theological school, and graduate school. After a most difficult day, he got to bed late; his wife had fallen asleep, and the phone rang and an angry voice said:

> "Listen, nigger, we've taken all we want from you. Before next week you'll be sorry you ever came to Montgomery." I hung up, but could not sleep. It seemed all my fears had come down on me at once. I had reached the saturation point.

King was ready to give up; he was exhausted. With courage almost gone, and at his kitchen table with a cup of coffee, King went to God in prayer. King spoke of his fear, the need of the people, and the realization that he could not do it alone. In that moment, King experienced the presence of the Divine and could sense an inner, quiet voice saying, "Stand up for righteousness, stand up for truth. God will be at your side forever."

AMID WAR, ECOLOGICAL DEVASTATION, AND WIDESPREAD VIOLENCE, WE MUST WORK FOR JUSTICE

- Justice is not a luxury, a philosophy, or an abstract ideology relegated to ivory towers.
- Justice begins with the vibrancy of our souls.
- Justice is an invitation to dance the dance of righteousness, of doing what is right by God and our neighbor.
- Justice means to realize standards of life in which we can live and grow together.

Considerations and Resources

- View the film documentary *Citizen King* or the movie *The Autobiography of Miss Jane Pittman*.
- Review various biblical and theological understandings of justice.
- "No Justice; No Peace" is a familiar chant sounded at protest marches. What does that phrase mean to you? What is the relationship between peace and justice?
- In what ways does the church support or hinder justice?
- What are some important justice issues in your town or city? How might your church or ministry become more involved?

My Thoughts and Ideas

_____

_____

_____

_____

_____

A Dancing Spirit

Kirk Byron Jones

Text
Psalm 51:10-15

Theme
To celebrate and encourage a dancing spirit.

Sermon Outline

CORETTA AND MARTIN DANCE

During their 1964 trip to Sweden to receive Dr. King's Nobel Peace Prize, Coretta and Martin danced at a ball held in Stockholm to celebrate the independence of Kenya:

> We and other members of our party were received as special guests, and the committee wanted Martin and me to dance the opening selection together. We had not danced since our college days in Boston. Martin had told me then that, as a Baptist, when he became pastor of a church, we would not be able to dance anymore in public because it would be distasteful to the older members of the congregation. We never had, and Martin was quite reluctant to dance now. The student committee begged and begged us, so we finally consented to waltz. It was great fun to be dancing again with Martin. (*My Life with Martin Luther King Jr.* [New York: Holt, Rinehart, and Winston, 1969], 15)

THERE IS A RELATIONSHIP BETWEEN DANCING AND DIVINITY

David imagines a free-spirited God in Psalm 51:12 (KJV). Imagining a free-spirited God who "moves in mysterious ways" invites us to have more of a dancing spirit.

MARTIN KING'S DANCING SPIRIT WAS EVIDENCED IN THREE WAYS

• King displayed a dancing oratorical style, "a dialogical dance" of sound and substance. His speech-making was a dance of clarity and grace.

• King saw faith in God and faithful human effort as two equally important "partners" in fashioning a more just society.

• King danced in his ability to "break free" from conventional thinking, especially in his courageous prophetic critique of the Vietnam War.

WE ARE ALL CALLED TO BE DANCING SPIRITS

In her book *Dancing Spirit: An Autobiography*, Judith Jamison, former star dancer of the Alvin Ailey American Dance Theatre, invokes the dancing spirit in us all:

> You don't have to be five feet ten to be a dancer. Don't let what your body does define what you can do. Think of movement as much bigger than what your body says you're limited to. Your hand can go into the depths of your heart to pull out what you need to communicate with another person. I made a career not on how high my legs were but on how high you *thought* they went. Dance is bigger than the physical body. Think bigger than that. When you extend your arm, it doesn't stop at the end of your fingers, because you're dancing bigger than that; you're dancing spirit. Take a chance. Reach out. Go further than you've ever gone before. ([New York: Doubleday, 1993], 264)

Considerations and Resources

• Before preaching about spirituality in dancing terms, think about how the majority in your congregation views dancing. Have a few pre-sermon conversations. This sermon cannot be comfortably preached in every church.

• Freedom, resurrection, and liberation are other theological themes that may be mentioned to justify understanding God in "a dancing way." What are some other themes?

• To witness the relationship between divinity and dance, attend any good dance recital, especially one by the legendary Alvin Ailey American Dance Theatre. Reflect personally and theologically on the spirituality of dance.

• Read the short but potent interpretation of King's life authored by Vincent Harding entitled *Martin Luther King, the Inconvenient Hero* (Maryknoll, N.Y.: Orbis Books, 1996). This will strengthen your understanding of King's prophetic witness.

My Thoughts and Ideas

_____

_____

_____

_____

_____

Week Three

Getting with God's New Thing

Kirk Byron Jones

Text

Isaiah 43:18-19

Theme

To stimulate anticipation and excitement over change and transformation.

Sermon Outline

RESISTING CHANGE

A cartoon showcased a baby chicken emerging from its shell, peering through binoculars at its new surroundings, and suddenly throwing away the binoculars and attempting to return to its shell. We are left to wonder what frightened the chicken so. Was it what it saw or what it could no longer see, both, or something else?

We have many reasons for resisting new changes.

EMBRACING CHANGE

The text offers three strategies for embracing change.

• Practice Holy Amnesia. "Do not remember the former things of old." Sometimes we have to forget to forge ahead.

• Practice Sacred Alertness. "Do you not perceive it?" Emptying ourselves of inhibitions involves filling ourselves with interest.

24

• Practice Divine Anticipation. "I will make a road in the wilderness."

Considerations and Resources

• We need to be alert not with the kind of hard vigilance that has us seeing the things we want to see, but with what Ellen Langer calls "soft vigilance" that has us on guard for the unexpected and the things that can only be seen in our peripheral vision.

• Miles Davis once wrote concerning his desire for musicians: "I wanted them to go beyond themselves. See, if you put a musician in a place where he has to do something different from what he does all the time, then he can do that; but he's got to think differently in order to do it" (Miles Davis with Quincy Troupe, *Miles, the Autobiography* [New York: Simon & Schuster, 1989], 220). Reflect theologically on this statement. What are its implications for this sermon?

• Consider using this sermon as the beginning of an envisioning process for the church in which the church begins to imagine freely new ministry thrusts and initiatives.

• Review *Necessary Losses* by Judith Viorst (New York: The Free Press, 1986). Viorst writes in the introduction: "For the road to human development is paved with renunciation. Throughout our life we grow by giving up" (p. 16).

My Thoughts and Ideas

_____

_____

_____

_____

_____

Change Your Thoughts

Charles Henry

Text

Proverbs 23:7

Theme

To challenge persons to move toward mental renewal.

Sermon Outline

WHO DO YOU THINK YOU ARE?

Your life depends on what you think. Change the way you think and you will change the way you are and the way the world responds to you.

THINK UP, NOT DOWN

- Look up for a new direction.
- Look up for a new motivation.
- Look up for a new perspective.

LOOK AHEAD, NOT BACK

- Learn from your failures.
- Don't let the past limit the future.
- Don't make precedents into predicaments.

LOOK IN, NOT OUT

- Where you have been is where you wanted to be.
- Where you go is where you'll take yourself.
- Who you become is whoever you want to be.

Considerations and Resources

• A plastic surgeon noticed that many of his patients seem to take on new personalities after their plastic surgery. In his book *Psycho-Cybernetics; A New Way to Get More Living out of Life* (Englewood, Cliffs, N.J.: Prentice-Hall, 1960), Maxwell Maltz attributed the entire phenomenon to what a person thinks of self. Today Maltz's thoughts are widely accepted as true. What we think, not only of ourselves but of everything around us, controls our outer look, our personalities, and our value systems. How do you know this to be true in your own life?

• Review Jesus' interactions with people. How much of his conversation was spent on getting people to see things in a different way?

• Read *A Lesson Before Dying* by Ernest Gaines Jr. (New York: A. A. Knopf, 1993). Note the connection drawn between self-belief and dignity.

My Thoughts and Ideas

_____

_____

_____

_____

_____

Week Four

Blurry Vision

Kirk Byron Jones

Text

1 Corinthians 13:8-13

Theme

To champion the fact that *dimly seeing* is still seeing.

Sermon Outline

WARNING SIGNS

Although most warning signs are in our bathrooms, many more of them are scattered about in various places around the house:

- "Flammable. Keep out of reach of children."
- "Causes eye irritation."
- "Do not use in cribs, beds, carriages and playpens."

These are warnings on items that we use every day.

There is a warning in our Scripture reading that is, interestingly enough, part of the Love chapter, often read at weddings. Though it is used as a wedding reading, Paul did not have brides and grooms *coming together* in mind when he wrote his eloquent, lyrical prose. Rather, he was concerned with church folk *coming apart*. Paul had founded the Christian community in Corinth and had left to organize churches elsewhere. It is five years later. The church has grown, and so have problems and tensions. One of the problems has to do with some at Corinth beginning to value

28

some spiritual gifts over others. Paul's response is to warn Corinth church members against valuing some gifts and some believers over others.

BLURRY VISION

It is in the context of this central warning against church division that Paul adds another warning. No doubt we often miss it in light of Paul's oratory on love, but the unsung warning is important. This usually unnoticed warning is the first phrase of verse 12. Remembering that Corinth had a large mirror manufacturing industry, and remembering that Jesus had a way of using ordinary people to plant the extraordinary inside of them, Paul says, "For now we see in a mirror, dimly" or "now we see but a poor reflection as in a mirror." Here is the warning: When it comes to God and the things of God, we all have burry vision.

I had my annual eye examination a few weeks ago. Initially when I was asked to read the chart with my old contact lenses in my eyes, I could barely make out the letters. I was not alarmed, because I knew my contact lenses needed to be replaced. They had become stained and blurred. As I'd thought, as soon as I was given a pair of new lenses, I could see clearly.

In that case, there was a remedy for my blurred vision. Paul says that we have blurred vision about God for which there is no remedy in this life. We have to wait until we experience God face to face to have our spiritual vision fully and finally cleared up; but for now, we have blurry vision.

OUR BLURRY VISION MAY ENCOURAGE US TO PRACTICE MORE HUMILITY

Since we all have blurry vision about God, no one knows all there is to know, and we need to learn from one another.

Some of the most wonderful insights about God can come from the most unexpected places. Never underestimate anybody, any place, any experience, any moment. On the one-year anniversary of September 11, I wanted to be careful that our nine-year-old didn't wake up to news stories that would sadden her at the beginning of the day. Somehow, I missed turning off the television in our room. I went in, and there she was watching news about the tragedy. I gently urged her to turn the television off and get dressed. I was concerned, and then something happened. After dressing, she went into the kitchen to make a sandwich. I noticed her pick up the mustard and begin making drawing-like motions. As I looked closer, I saw she was making a smiley face on her sliced ham. I smiled. I asked her why she made it. She responded, "Oh I do this all the time." All the time she makes her joy and her gladness even when the news around her is sad.

OUR BLURRY VISION MAY INSPIRE ADVENTURESOME FAITH

Since we don't ever see all about God, there is always more to be discovered and experienced.

I fear that our faith experience is more burdensome than adventuresome. Part of the problem is our addiction to sameness. Why is it in church that we say and do many of the same things in exactly the same way, over and over and over again? Predictability and habit can snuff the life out of a believer and a church. They are the two great enemies, silent killers, of adventuresome faith, or what Derrick Bell calls "evolving faith" (in *Ethical Ambition: Living a Life of Meaning and Worth* [London: Bloomsbury, 2002]).

Blurry vision is not about being able to see; it is about wanting to see more. It is about hungering, thirsting, and yearning to see that new truth leads to new growth.

Considerations and Resources

• Blurry vision is a physical problem for many. How can you preach about having blurry vision spiritually without offending people who suffer with vision problems?

• "Amazing Grace," one of the great songs of the faith, has the lyric, "I was blind, but now I see" (written by John Newton, ca. 1779). Reconcile the gift of spiritual sight with sacred blurry vision.

• Paul's conversion experience involved his sight. Perhaps his experience can inform this sermon in some way.

My Thoughts and Ideas

_____

_____

_____

_____

_____

Our Spiritual Enemies

Charles Henry

Text

Ephesians 6:10-12

Theme

To revisit the biblical theme of Satan and spiritual evil, and to wrestle with its reality for our time.

Sermon Outline

WE ARE FIGHTING AGAINST THE EVIL OF PRINCIPALITIES AND POWERS

- The satanic kingdom is highly organized.
- Evil is a powerful destructive force.
- The battle is for ultimate control over our thoughts and attitudes.

WE WRESTLE

- We are supported with the "whole armor of God."
- We are supported by the knowledge that evil is ultimately a defeated foe.
- We are supported by God's undisputed victory over evil in Jesus.

Considerations and Resources

- Some may find your preaching about Satan to be out of date. How can you preach about evil in such a way that even the most ardent skeptics will understand (1) why the early church leaders spoke of evil as represented by Satan, and (2) why this thematic emphasis is important today?

• Are racism, slavery, and segregation examples of "satanic evil"?

• Summarize and review your own theology of the presence of evil in the world. How did you come to this understanding? What are your experiential and theological resources?

• Political rhetoric, even from the highest sources, is not beyond characterizing other nations and causes as "evil." What are the dangers of fixating on the evil of "others"?

• Flip Wilson, a legendary comedian, popularized the phrase, "The devil made me do it." What is the truth and falsehood in such a statement? How do you balance formidable influence with personal accountability? Your answers to these questions may lead to an entire series, entitled "The Devil Made Me Do It: True or False?"

My Thoughts and Ideas

_____

_____

_____

_____

_____

This Will Preach!

Gilbert H. Caldwell

The following texts ought to attract the prayerful thinking and praying of all who preach in the African American church.

1. "And now do not be distressed, or angry with yourselves, because you sold me here; for God sent me before you to preserve life" (Genesis 45:5). Some prefer a rendering that says in stark terms: "You meant it for evil, but God meant it for good." The words from the conversation Joseph had with his brothers who sold him into slavery are an essential ingredient in the conversation that black Americans (C. Eric Lincoln's term) must have with white America. The enslaved (for any reason) must become God's "wounded healers," healers not only of themselves, but of those who inflicted the wounds. These words, in this post-Katrina time, are appropriate for the poor among us as they speak to their middle- and upper-class black sisters and brothers. We who believe we have "arrived" are in need of being in such proximity to the poor—black and otherwise—that they can ease or absolve us of the guilt we must accept for being responsible for some portions of their poverty. "Benign neglect" is not an unknown reality for those of us in the African American middle class.

2. "How could we sing the LORD's / song in a foreign land?" (Psalm 137:4). Where are the Spirituals of this racially integrated generation? What are the songs that emerged out of the experience of being what our fathers and mothers could never be? Of going where they could never go. Of doing what they could never do. And of having incomes and houses and cars that they could never dream of having? The Lord's song sung in a foreign land is never so heavenly centered that it is of no earthly good. How do we sing about the signs of the kingdom that we have and are seeking to build on earth?

3. "But those who wait for the LORD shall renew their strength, / they shall mount up with wings like eagles, / they shall run and not be weary, / they shall walk and not faint" (Isaiah 40:31). I am a living witness to the power of these words when repeated over and over again as I lay flat on my back in the darkness of a hospital room. I was in that situation twice within the period of a month. The first time was the removal of a nonmalignant brain tumor. The second time, I was hospitalized due to an infection that developed during the first operation. Preachers are not good *wait-ers*. We may be good at fulfilling the role of "serving" the food of the gospel in our preaching and our teaching, but sometimes going one-on-one with God in the dark loneliness of a hospital room taxes the meaning of the words that we sometimes too easily offer to others. But something happens in the waiting that validates what we have claimed to believe. It is not us but God who gives us the strength, the wings like eagle wings, the endurance to run the race without tiring, and the capacity to "walk the walk" that we have talked so much about. The "something that happens" may not be a return to physical health, but the greater "happening" is the recovery or the first-time discovery of the God within us who sent Jesus to lead us.

4. "I am black and beautiful. . . . Do not gaze at me because I am dark, / because the sun has gazed on me" (Song of Songs 1:5). There is a myth that speaks of the sexual prowess of black males. Some of us spend a lifetime seeking to live up to that myth. But the African American preacher—female or male—has an opportunity to "rescue" the Song of Songs (or Song of Solomon) from its nonuse and misuse. The pulpit should have been and ought to be the locus for preaching and teaching the "sexual healing" that Marvin Gaye sang about. The Song of Songs is a place to begin.

Skin color, hair texture, and body configurations are affirmed mightily in the Song of Songs. There is a commercial for soap that features real, full-size women. They ought to have one that features full-size men. On hair, my grandmother, Mama Irene, used to say that "good hair" is any hair that covers your head. I don't know whether Bishop T. D. Jakes in his "Woman, Thou Art

Loosed" programming addresses body and sexuality, but whether he does or not, the African American pulpit must.

Recently on TV I heard a woman therapist say that the contradiction of our society is that we value monogamy in our relationships but that we are shy about teaching sexual diversity in our monogamous sexual activity. Should not the preacher proclaim that church folk have been liberated from practicing only the "missionary position" in our sex lives? Demythologizing that concept makes for interesting preaching and teaching. Our inauthentic anti-homosexual pronouncements seem to provide "cover" for our cautious and unsure beliefs about heterosexual liberation. If we dared, conversations about same-gender sexual activity could be a platform for deeper teaching and preaching about sexuality and sexual activity.

February

FEBRUARY

AFRICAN AMERICAN HERITAGE MONTH

Sermon Outlines

Week One

Fearless Listening

Kirk Byron Jones

Text

Luke 2:41-46

Theme

To promote attentiveness to and ownership of one's own voice as well as of the authentic voices of others.

Sermon Outline

FEARLESS SPEAKING

Lilyan Wilder has written a book entitled *7 Steps to Fearless Speaking* (New York: J. Wiley, 1999). The book offers ways to conquer the fear of speaking in public, a fear that makes itself known in many different ways, including in fearing you'll go blank, lose your place, and make a fool of yourself.

As important as *fearless speaking* is, *fearless listening* is no less important. What is fearless listening?

FEARLESS LISTENING IN THE TEMPLE AND OUR LIVES

• The teachers in the temple were not afraid to listen to a new voice and a new vision.

- They listened though the voice was young.
- They listened though the voice was inexperienced.
- Jesus was not afraid to listen to his voice growing louder and louder inside him.
- Fred Craddock has written, "To this point, all signs of Jesus' special nature or mission have been to or through others: the angel, Mary, Elizabeth, Zechariah, shepherds, Simeon, and Anna, but now he claims it for himself" (*Luke* [Louisville, Ky.: John Knox Press, 1990], 42).
- Jesus grew into his full voice.
- We are called to grow into our full voice.

Considerations and Resources

- Listen to the voices in the book/CD package, *Say it Plain: A Century of Great African American Speeches,* edited by Catherine Ellis and Stephen Drury Smith (New York: W. W. Norton & Co., 2005).
- Note qualities of familiar voices in your life.
- What are the distinctive features of your own voice?
- Offer a response to the following quote by Emile Zola: "If you asked what I came into this world to do, I will tell you: I came to live out loud."
- What prevents us from hearing our own voice and from hearing the voices of others?

My Thoughts and Ideas

From Strength to Strength

Marsha Brown Woodward

Text

Psalm 84:5-7

Theme

To see life as a process of growing stronger.

Sermon Outline

POWER AND POSSIBILITY

I often go back to the scene from the movie *Roots* during which Kunta Kinte raises his new baby and says that the only thing greater is the universe. This picture of power and possibility was a contradiction to the reality of being enslaved. Your situation does not describe your personhood. Even in confinement one can be free. These slaves who had been strong, free, self-determining people found a new strength borne out of the pains of separation and had a hope for the future to pass on to the next generation. They were a strong people becoming stronger in the midst of adversity.

THE PSALMIST MAKES AN AUDACIOUS STATEMENT

The wilderness is transformed to bounty as this people pass through. It is not weakness that has brought them to this difficult place but their strength. From this challenging time they will become stronger.

41

Paradox As a Way of Life

• Play with the paradox in the passage; how do you handle the seeming contradictions of the normal thinking process? We often tend to think in terms of opposites (such as weak vs. strong) and give the impression that one must always move within that framework; but here it is declared that both places are strength. To rename the wilderness as a place of bounty is to recast the wilderness experience.

• I remember when I first came to understand that challenges came to Job because he had been faithful. God believed that Job could be trusted to endure great distress because of how he had lived. Job was a strong person. And at the end, Job was an even stronger person. He knew more about God than he did before his challenges. Job went not from weakness to strength but from strength to strength.

• What is your testimony of moving from strength to strength? Remembering our experience nurtures confidence to trust God in the future.

In a Wilderness? Transform It.

• The paradox of our faith is that in the midst of seasons during which we appear to be defeated, we can still be used by God to change the environment. Throughout Joseph's life, a repeated phrase was "and God was with Joseph." Sold into slavery, he made Potiphar's house a better place. Thrown into prison, he made the prison a better place and helped others who were incarcerated as well. His dream was placed on hold, deferred, and yet he did not wallow in the pain or claim *victimness.*

• What are the historical strengths of the African American community, especially the African American Christian community? In what ways are these strengths being claimed or not claimed by the community you are serving? Does it make a difference when people see themselves moving out of a place of strength to strength rather than from a place of weakness to strength? Would it make a difference in your life if you saw the challenges in your life as the result of strengths and not as a pun-ishment for weakness? Can a congregation see itself as weak? Would it be different if the collective mind-set of the congregation were that of strength?

• Coming together makes change more possible. In the mid-1940s, a woman in Virginia refused to give up her seat on a bus in a manner very similar to that of Rosa Parks. The case didn't go very far, because there was little community support. But a seed was planted, and over the years it was nurtured. Finally, the day arrived when Rosa Parks's refusal to move ignited a movement that shook the world. This time the community came together. The community built on its own strengths and, in time, trans-formed not just Montgomery, but the nation.

Considerations and Resources

• The sermon works with the challenge to think outside the box by moving away from polar thinking, such as opposites and either/or thinking. In what specific ways does this kind of think-ing limit life? How has it limited your life as a person and as a minister?

• Consider using more evidence from the Joseph saga.

• Reggie McNeal's book *A Work of Heart: Understanding How God Shapes Spiritual Leaders* (San Francisco: Jossey-Bass, 2000) is helpful in seeing the process of transformation we must go through in order to become more like Christ.

• If you include a children's moment in your worship, you might consider the story *Elmer in the Snow* by David McKee (New York: HarperCollins, 2004). Elmer, a patchwork ele-phant, helps his friends understand the relativity of words such as *cold* and *hot*. For example, when they complain of the heat of the jungle, he takes them to a mountaintop with snow and cold, and when they return, the warmth is not such a bad thing any longer.

• Review the lyrics of Darryl Coley's song, "I'll Be with You."

My Thoughts and Ideas

_____

_____

_____

_____

_____

Week Two

Mighty Causes Are Calling Us

Marsha Brown Woodward

Text

Isaiah 61:1-4

Theme

To reaffirm God's call to transformation.

Sermon Outline

GOD'S CALL IS A CONTINUING CALL

W. E. B. Dubois, in the early part of the twentieth century, and Martin Luther King Jr., toward the end of the twentieth century, challenged their generations to stretch toward a higher vision, to see a world larger than the one in which they were living.

> Give us grace, O God, to dare to do the deed which we well know cries to be done. Let us not hesitate because of ease, or the words on men's mouths, or our own lives. Mighty causes are calling us—the freeing of women, the training of children, the putting down of hate and murder and poverty—all these and more. But they call with voices that mean work and sacrifice and death. Mercifully grant us, O God, the spirit of Esther, that we say: "I will go unto the King and if I perish, I perish." Amen. (W. E. B. DuBois, *Prayers for Dark People* [Amherst: University of Massachusetts Press, 1980], 21)

> So, I conclude by saying again today that we have a task and let us go out with a "divine dissatisfaction." Let us be dissatisfied

45

until America will no longer have a high blood pressure of creeds and an anemia of deeds. Let us be dissatisfied until the tragic walls that separate the outer city of wealth and comfort and the inner city of poverty and despair shall be crushed by the battering rams of the forces of justice. (From "Where Do We Go from Here?" Southern Christian Leadership Conference presidential address, 1967, printed in *A Testament of Hope: The Essential Writings of Martin Luther King, Jr.*, ed. James Melvin Washington [San Francisco: HarperSanFrancisco, 1991], 251.

THE UNPOPULARITY OF MIGHTY CAUSES

Large numbers are not necessarily an indication of the work. Since there is the possibility for pain, humiliation, and sacrifice, many will be content with something less than God's best. Crowds have their place such as the March on Washington, but the test was in the smaller marches after which many ended up in jail, beaten, or bruised. What is the cost to be faithful?

LONG-HAUL LIVING

• The people of Montgomery demonstrate long-haul living. Paint a mental picture of the months of walking and sharing rides in the cold of winter as well as in the heat of summer. In their story we see the embodiment of the Isaiah passage.

• Myles Horton and the Highlander Center demonstrate long-haul living. Bringing interracial groups together in the same place for study in the 1940s and 1950s in the mountains of Tennessee was phenomenal. They risked their lives for the belief that different groups could work and live together.

• Beyers Naudé in South Africa is a sign of long-haul living. He was working to end apartheid when it was not popular and was sharing in the transformation of the nation.

• Ella Baker, Septima Clark, Fannie Lou Hamer, and countless others were the visionaries of the civil rights struggle and believed more in the vision than in their own personal recognition. They epitomized long-haul living in the multitude of sacrifices that they made.

WE ARE CALLED TO TRANSFORM

• Isaiah's passage is more descriptive than the frequently quoted Luke passage. What can the church learn from change theories and work that has been done to help others learn to accept change? Consider developing a theology of change.

• If for freedom we have been set free, what is the work still yet to be done? Generational cycles of abuse and addiction, a seeming disdain for education held by many, and an appearance of holding values antithetical to the kingdom all speak to the need for transformed thinking. How do we capture a vision that inspires people today for long-haul living?

• Since God could change the world in an instant and make people act right, and since God knows better than anyone else that humans have a track record for choosing the opposite of his plan, why on earth does God insist on including the people of God in the very work of transformation? God seems to trust us (humans) more than we trust God.

Considerations and Resources

• Consider a movie night and show a film that will stimulate a discussion around the hard work of working for change in society. *The Long Walk Home* is a good possibility, but there are many others. Seek out films that include ordinary people.

• *Freedom's Daughter* is another resource that tells the story of women in the work of transformation.

• Before preaching, reflect first on your community and second on the world. What areas are you being called to work on? Congregations are gifted to do certain parts of the work of transformation. What is the gift that you and the congregation bring to the wider family?

• Children's Moment: Currently, there is a commercial for a mobile phone company that focuses on the phrase, "Can you hear me now?" Ask children what does it mean to hear and what helps hearing be clear. How can we hear God and one another better?

My Thoughts and Ideas

God Loves You Madly

Kirk Byron Jones

Text

Lamentations 3:22-23

Theme

To embrace and enjoy the extravagant love of God.

Sermon Outline

MAD, RENEWING LOVE

- Duke Ellington had this expression he would offer his audience after each performance on behalf of himself and his extraordinary band. He would smile a brilliant smile and say, as if he were saying it for the very first time, "We love you madly."
- The Hebrew root word for *compassion, mercy* derives from the Hebrew word meaning "womb." The writer speaks of God as a loving mother who loves her child with the intensity of that love constantly renewing itself: new mercies!
- One of the great things about the text is that it challenges false notions of God that we receive when we are young, that we spend a lifetime getting and that some of us never get over. There are phrases we hear that paint God out to be this great wrathful Judge whom we need to be afraid of because:
  o "God doesn't like ugly."
  o "God's gonna get you."
  o "Be careful; God's watching."
  o "God's going to punish you."

FRESH AND NEW EACH MORNING

Since God's mercy—God's mad love—is there fresh and new each morning, we do well to receive it afresh and anew each morning, or somewhere along the course of our day.

One needs to discover ways of soulfully receiving God's new mercies each day. Find a way; find many ways. There is a small stained glass hanging in my office at home that comes alive when the sun hits it every morning. When you look at it, you see a richly blue pond surrounded on each side by bands of purple and white flowers. In the middle, a stream of water flows freely down into the pond. One of my ways of receiving God's new mercies is mentally standing under that stream and receiving into my spirit its refreshing, renewing waters.

Considerations and Resources

- How have you experienced God's love in your life?
- Create your own way of visualizing God's love.
- Reflect on Duke Ellington's quote.

My Thoughts and Ideas

_____

_____

_____

_____

_____

Week Three

Greatness Is Not a Requirement

Marsha Brown Woodward

Text

Acts 1:12-15; 2:43-47

Theme

God uses and chooses ordinary people to do extraordinary things.

Sermon Outline

OUR SOCIETY LIKES SUPERSTARS

Everywhere you look there are stars. List outstanding sports figures, entertainers, and politicians, both historical and current. Even in the community of faith we often give the impression that big is better and that the pastor of a mega-congregation is more sought after than the pastor of a small congregation.

• What is the cost of being great? Who defines great?

• Could it be possible that we don't attempt new things for God because we believe that we aren't good enough?

• Could the need for greatness be keeping us from an experience that would change not only us but also the world in which we live?

JESUS WAS AN EQUAL-OPPORTUNITY, AFFIRMATIVE-ACTION EMPLOYER

Consider the diversity of those who followed Jesus, the Twelve, and also the larger group. Who were the 120 in the upper room, and how many were named? Were the unnamed less important? All were commissioned to change the world.

They were chosen not *because of* but *in spite of.*

Jesus chose a motley crew to have the responsibility for taking the gospel to the world. Together they could do what they could not do separately. They needed a special strength and power to fulfill this responsibility. They were chosen to demonstrate a new model to the world.

Greatness is not needed for the work of the kingdom.

We need not be great to work for justice. We need not be great to provide food and clothing, tutor, and mentor. Countless African Americans have made valuable contributions and received little recognition: Charles Hamilton Houston who taught at Howard University law school and was the force behind Thurgood Marshall and the lawyers of that generation; inventors such as Charles Drew; schoolteachers and preachers. All these have changed lives without making headlines.

FAITHFULNESS NOT GREATNESS

It is not greatness that we need, but faithfulness. If we yield to God, God will be able to use us to do extraordinary things. The 120 were faithful to what Jesus had spoken, and there were great results. Where is God calling the collective body today to come to one accord? What might God want to do through us?

Considerations and Resources

• More than just being humble, faithfulness is a challenge to believe that one can be used by God to do extraordinary things.

What beliefs might need to be unlearned in order to relearn kingdom values?

• Are there individuals in the congregation who have had significant effect on the lives of others in the community but have received little recognition?

• Review the seven aspects or realities of our relationship with God in *Experiencing God: How to Live the Full Adventure of Knowing and Doing the Will of God* (Nashville: Broadman & Holman Publishers, 1994) by Henry Blackaby and Claude King. This could be a good book to read before the sermon or to consider using as a follow-up with the entire congregation or with a small group desiring to grow in their relationship.

• If you include a time with children, an activity with stars might be a fun way to encourage them to think about greatness. Many children will be able to name someone they think is great. Children can be encouraged to do things together that will be of help to others.

My Thoughts and Ideas

Now-Faith

Marsha Brown Woodward

Text

Hebrews 11:1

Theme

Faith is not just for the past but also for today.

Sermon Outline

DISCONNECTED WORDS

Imagine for a moment that you are defining the first two words in this verse separately: *Now* and *Faith*. First, think of all the ways that faith is defined and what it entails to have faith. One of the meanings has to do with embracing the "not yet" as if it "really were."

Take the first word of the verse, *now*, and do the same thing. Think of all the ways that *now* is defined. *Now* implies a current experience, real time and place. *Now* indicates that one is speaking in the present tense, that something can be seen, held, or touched in the here and now.

Putting *faith* and *now* together appears to be a problem. It is putting *not yet* with *actually is*. There appears to be a disconnect when *now* and *faith* are placed together.

UNRESOLVED ISSUES

We live in the contemporary now with many issues that are not resolved. Racism, sexism, ageism, and too many other "isms" leave us with more questions than answers. Economic challenges are found in every community, and the questions of a just wage and fair employment are as real today as at any time in history. In the contemporary now, there often appear to be too many mountains that are too high to climb. We are called to live our questions, and that takes faith.

NOW-FAITH

Our challenge, as it was for our biblical sisters and brothers, is to have *Now-Faith*. In my now-moment, I need faith to believe that God is doing a new thing. In the now of unanswered questions and unresolved situations, there is a need for faith. Now-Faith is the challenge for people today in order to have the courage to work to change the injustice in society. To live in the now by faith is to be radically dependent on God. Listening for God, sensing the scent of God, following the path on which God is leading takes Now-Faith. Becoming the contemporary Abraham, midwives (Shiphrah and Puah), Rahab, Ruth, Esther, and Mordacai takes Now-Faith. Becoming the contemporary Sojourner Truth, W. E. B. DuBois, Septima Clark, Bernice Johnson Reagan, and Martin Luther King Jr. takes Now-Faith.

Considerations and Resources

The familiarity of the text will have many thinking that they already know what you will say. Using just two words from the first verse will create a new curiosity and sensitivity for an old text.

• This is a great passage for a significant anniversary in the life of a congregation. You can use those who have given time, energy, and commitment to the work and extend a challenge to the next generation to continue the legacy.

• Use appropriate songs that trumpet faith. How might our singing affect our living? Recall the role of singing in the civil rights movement. Singing, the words, the beat, and the act build Now-Faith.

• If you include a moment with children, introduce them to mustard seeds and how small they are and yet how much power we have if we only have faith the size of a mustard seed.

- There are many examples of practical powerful Now-Faith in autobiographies and biographies. You will find many great stories of Now-Faith in the following books:
  - *Barbara Jordan: American Hero* by Mary Beth Rogers (New York: Bantam Books, 1998)
  - *Some of Us Did Not Die: New and Selected Essays of June Jordan* by June Jordan (New York: Basic/Civitas Books, 2002)
  - *Faith in Time: The Life of Jimmy Scott* by David Ritz (Cambridge, Mass.: Da Capo Press, 2002)
  - *With Head and Heart* by Howard Thurman (New York: Harcourt Brace Jovanovich, 1979)
  - *Stride Toward Freedom: The Montgomery Story* by Martin Luther King Jr. (New York: Harper, 1958)

My Thoughts and Ideas

_____

_____

_____

_____

_____

A Season of Transformation

Marsha Brown Woodward

Texts

Ecclesiastes 3:4 (1-8); Isaiah 61:3-7 (1-11)

Theme

To celebrate Lent as a season of sacred change and transformation.

Sermon Outline

A SEASON FOR CHANGE

The writer of Ecclesiastes reminds us that life is a series of seasons and that we will each experience this variety in our lives. There will be times of joy and sorrow, endings, and peace and chaos. In each of these seasons we have the opportunity to grow; and while the writer does not use the word *transformation*, there are times in our lives when we are in a season of transformation. Lent is a season in which we can experience transformation. It is a time when we can experience the presence and power of God in ways that will be life-changing for ourselves and for this community of faith.

TRANSFORMATION SIGNS

These special times in our lives are often really multiple seasons. You may experience the seasons of preparation, waiting, anticipation, unknowns, wilderness, exile, or renewal. Although you probably won't experience all of them, transformation occurs after one has journeyed through several of these seasons, occasionally in a short period of time, but often over an extended period of months or years. It is a season during which you know deep within that God is working and that you must go through this season to get to the next place that God has for you on your journey. It is a hard place, one with many unknowns, and yet one that we don't want to abandon, because we are learning things about God and about our relationship with God that we can discover nowhere else.

Lent may be that time of transformation, or a season that helps us understand transformation as we reflect again on the life and ministry of Jesus.

- Jesus is baptized by John and then is led by the spirit into the wilderness.
- Jesus stays in the wilderness for forty days and at the end is tempted by Satan.
- Jesus resists the temptation and has new power and from this new place preaches his first sermon.

Like Jesus, we, too, experience times of preparation that let us know that something is about to happen, that our equilibrium is being disturbed. Although we may not be led into an actual place that looks like a wilderness, we may in fact enter a life wilderness, which feels barren and dry.

SELF-EXAMINATION

The passage from Ecclesiastes invites us to a time of self-reflection and examination.

- Where are you now, where have you been, and how have you experienced the seasons of life?
- Have you seen these seasons as burdens or impositions?

• Has it been your desire to skip over some seasons, wanting to experience only the *good* or *easy;* or have you been opened to the challenging and hard seasons as well?

Attitude can affect our experience, and the writer of the scripture in some ways was trying to help the first hearers gain perspective.

Considerations and Resources

• Include information on the history and background of Lent. The websites www.cresourcei.org and www.crivoice.org have basic information on the church year and how certain seasons are celebrated.

• Encourage members of the congregation to keep a journal during the Lenten season. If they start this habit now, they have a good chance of keeping it after Lent is over.

• As members prepare for the Lenten season, encourage them to ask, "What will enable me to serve God more fully?" In this way, whether they give up something or begin something, it will be for the purpose of growing as disciples of Christ. For example, they might give up an hour of television in order to take up an hour of reading the Bible, or they might give up buying coffee at work in order to give that amount to a mission project.

• If you do a special Bible study for the Lenten season, consider looking at people who change or experience change in Scripture, such as Ruth, Esther, Job, Jonah, Paul, Mary Magdalene, and Zaccheus.

• Include a time of sharing or testimony during the service or even during the sermon. Invite people to turn and share with those behind them a time when they have been transformed during a difficult season.

• If you have a children's moment, talk about the season of Lent and what it means to different people. If you still have ashes from your Ash Wednesday service, you could have them for the children and talk about how they are a symbol of being sorry for things you have done wrong. A second symbol might be a tambourine to represent joy. Together, the ashes and tambourine remind us that there are times when we are sorry and sad and times when we are happy. Some children may be open to sharing times when they have been sorry and times when they have been happy and joyful.

• How can Lent be a time of reflection and introspection for individuals in your congregation? How can Lent be a season of introspection for the congregation as a whole?

My Thoughts and Ideas

_____

_____

_____

_____

_____

Loving God; Loving Large

Cheryl Kirk-Duggan

Text

Genesis 1:26, 31; Song of Songs 1:5

Theme

Love is our context for life, a daily act of praise, honoring God and ourselves in spiritual, emotional, physical, psychological, economic, and pleasurable ways.

Sermon Outline

INTRODUCE THE TWO TEXTS AND SAY WHY THEY ARE IMPORTANT FOR HEALTHY DISCIPLESHIP

- To love, to know *agape, filia,* and *eros* is to be in complete intimacy with God.
- To love God is to love yourself and your neighbor, for both are made in God's image.
- To love large is to be open to the blessings of God in Communion and community.
- To love God and to love large is to love your own blackness as a gift of God.

LOVING GOD: OUR CONTEXT FOR LIVING

- We are made in God's image and thus embody the goodness of God.
- To acknowledge our sacredness is not idolatry, but superb stewardship.
- That we are given dominion means we are given stewardship in trust.

- Stewardship is the freedom and responsibility of being just in our use of human and financial resources and moral capital.
- Loving God and ourselves is our vocation, our call to life on planet earth.

LOVING LARGE: OUR ATTITUDE AND MODUS OPERANDI FOR DAILY LIFE, IN PRAISE TO GOD

- To love large is an opportunity and a challenge that answers the question, "What would Jesus do?"
- To love large is to acknowledge our own levels of woundedness and the need for healing.
- To love large is to be open to having people who love us in our lives and to stay away from those who abuse us.
- To love large is to love every part of ourselves, without exception.
- To love large is an opportunity to celebrate our blackness, femaleness, and godliness.
- To love large helps us have an attitude of joy, not of victim, as God's plan for us.
- To love large involves acknowledgement (confession), an attitude adjustment, and action.

Considerations and Resources

- This sermon seeks to place love of God and love of personhood on equal ground. To deliver this sermon effectively, the preacher needs to be thoroughly convinced of the sacredness of self-love. One of the greatest recent stories of the journey to self-love is Alice Walker's *The Color Purple* (New York: Harcourt Brace Jovanovich, 1982).
- Consider reading this classic or seeing the film in preparation to deliver this message. Consider quoting from Baby Suggs' classic sermon in Toni Morrison's *Beloved* ([New York; Alfred A. Knopf, 1987], 88-89).
- Reflect on this quote by Ireneaus, an early church father: "The glory of God is a living [person]" (*Against Heresies*, book 4, chap. 20, sec. 7).

My Thoughts and Ideas

_____

_____

_____

_____

_____

MARCH

Looking Back at Fifty-plus Years of Preaching

Gilbert H. Caldwell

A Confession

In preparing this material for the book, I have been as involved or more so than I was involved in my sermon preparation for much of my ministry. Placing the seat of my pants in the seat of a chair and beginning with prayer and then allowing God, my muse, to take over, brings me a kind of joy that the busyness of my active ministry did not provide. My wish for you, my younger colleagues, is that you will find the job of reading, preparation, writing, thinking, and creating while you are still active in ministry, as I am now finding in retirement in my seventies!

Some Things I Now Wish I Had Done

1. Find my own "preaching voice" rather than bemoaning the fact that I did not have the preaching gifts of others. Imitation of others may be a form of flattery to them, but it fails to use the gifts God has given us.

2. Be less concerned about stimulating emotion in my listeners and more concerned about encouraging them to "blend" content, emotion, intellect, and "mother wit" that is within them and hopefully is evoked by my preaching.

3. Experiment, experiment, experiment! I was a manuscript, an outline, and sometimes a "without notes" Preacher. I never found what was best for me, and I regretted that. I should have rejoiced in that and relished my experimentation, believing that congregations deserve not only fresh content each Sunday, but also different ways of delivering the content.

4. Use silence more! Not only deliberately creating "pregnant pauses" in the sermon (often they deliver no offspring/no issue),

but deliberate, intentional, directed silence that helps the preacher and the people in the pew be "at home" in their silence. Howard Thurman was a divine-directed master in the use of silence.

5. Have sermon talkbacks! Some of my colleagues tell me this is a no-no in the Black Church. I am not sure that I have understood what they meant. Were they saying that talkback provides opportunity for disagreement, which should never happen? Were they saying that the intent of the sermon is compromised when there are opportunities for reflection? Whatever! Sermon talkback with guidelines for discussion is something I would do more frequently if I had it to do over again!

6. Explore the history/tradition of mysticism. Resources for exploring Christian mysticism are many. Howard Thurman was my favorite mystic. I heard him at Marsh Chapel at Boston University and took the course Spiritual Disciplines with him, a course I wish I could now retake. I was not ready for it in 1957, but now I am. "A mystic is anyone who has the gnawing suspicion that the apparent discord, brokenness, contradictions, and discontinuities that assault us every day might conceal a hidden unity. It is a [sense of] Oneness in which all things . . . are . . . annihilated. [What remains is God]" (*The Beliefnet Guide to Kabbalah*, by Arthur Goldwag [New York: Three Leaves Press, 2005], x). It is not desertion of the Christian faith to explore and learn from Zen Buddhism, the Sufi tradition of Islam, and Judaism's Kabbalah!

7. Finally, some tongue-in-cheek comments. I would now not be jealous of my brothers and sisters who have the capacity to offer the gift of song from the pulpit, even though I don't have that capacity. I would continue to enjoy all forms of preaching, whooping and all, but not get jealous at the response from the congregation some get, when too often I got none at all. I would seek not to imitate what is said about us as preachers: "Preachers will fly across the country to preach a sermon, but will not walk across the street to hear one." I would challenge the saying: "A preacher is too often invisible

during the week and incomprehensible on Sunday" by working at visibility and vision, both during the week and on Sunday. Instead, the church, with its sometimes-shaky voice, is called to sing, knowing that in time the walls will come tumbling down.

MARCH

SERMON OUTLINES

Are You a Person God Can Trust?

Marsha Brown Woodward

Text

Job 1:8

Theme

God desires to trust us with tasks, visions, and other assignments.

Sermon Outline

CAN GOD TRUST YOU?

Have you ever asked yourself the question, "Can God trust me?" or "Would God select me to be used as an example of someone who could be depended upon to be faithful even in the midst of testing?" If Satan were to approach God today as he did in Job's day, would you be a candidate for being selected by God to stand up under severe testing?

Retell the beginning of the book of Job. (*The Message* offers a good paraphrase.) Highlight that Satan comes to God and says there is no one who can be found who will be faithful. God responds by asking, "Have you considered my servant Job?" Not convinced, Satan returns, and God again replies, "Have you considered my servant Job?"

BEING TRUSTED BY GOD IS NOT AN EASY ASSIGNMENT

- Job experiences great loss.
- Job finds himself in a very difficult place. Being trusted by God is not a guarantee that one will be exempted from the challenges of life. Instead, the opposite often is true; one will experience hardship and great difficulty.

CAN GOD TRUST YOU?

- Can God trust you to be the salt, the light, and the leaven that is needed for this world?
- Can God trust you to be more loving?
- Can God trust you to wait?
- Can God trust you to listen?

God is looking for women and men, girls and boys in this generation that he can trust. God is not looking for perfect people, but for those who will be committed to the kingdom. Would God say, "Have you considered my servant _____ (fill in your name)?" if God's reputation was being challenged?

Considerations and Resources

- Consider a time of commitment and dedication following the sermon. Here is a prayer that can be made available:

Dear God,

I am glad to have the assurance that I can always trust in you. You are the changeless God, the same yesterday, today, and tomorrow. I am grateful that you are always there for me, but I am learning that you also want to be able to trust me. In every generation you look for women and men, girls and boys that you can trust. I want to be that kind of person. God, day by day, grow me into a person that you can trust with a vision, a dream, or an opportunity to witness. Help me be the one who you can say will show up, stand out, and speak for you.

God, I cannot do this of my own strength and power, but I believe you are able to do a great work in and through me. So from this day forward, please do whatever you must in my life to help me in becoming a person you can trust. Amen.

• Trust is important, but equally important is knowing when and whom not to trust. Consider addressing the tensions Job might have had by trusting God. Job trusted God more than his relationships with his friends or with others in the community.

• What would it look like for a congregation to be trusted by God? What greater vision might God be calling the collective community to during this Lenten season?

• Lent is a time for reflection on our relationship with Jesus. Focus on the importance of relationship to both God and Jesus. During these six weeks, encourage the congregation to examine their relationship. What state is it in? Would they describe it as growing or stagnant?

• If you include a moment with children during your worship experience, consider using this same theme, but use a different story to focus on trust. Another possibility is to have a chair and ask the children what it is used for (hopefully someone will respond that it is used to sit on). Then you can ask whether they worry about how much they weigh or if the chair will hold them, and so on. Generally, they will be able to grasp that they trust that the chair will hold them because that is what chairs do. Likewise, we trust God because God has promised to support us.

My Thoughts and Ideas

_____

_____

_____

_____

Clothed for the Journey

Marsha Brown Woodward

Text

Mark 6:7-13

Theme

To observe how our minds, attitudes, and values become our new clothes.

Sermon Outline

WE ARE CALLED TO BE NEW

If we have been baptized into Christ, we have become like Christ and are now clothed liked him. Clothes are a symbol of our mind-set, our attitudes, and our values; a sign that we do things like Christ. No longer from a human point of view, we are now striving to think and act like Christ. This new worldview is an ongoing challenge. We live in a world that often neglects to help us distinguish its view.

It is also true that many times we subtly try to downplay the importance of the Christian worldview because we say that it really cannot be lived out or that it was for that time in history when Scripture was written or some other time in history, which is a way of implying that it is not for the time in which we live. We are called daily to give our lives and to allow our minds to be transformed. Lent is a time when we pray that God will transform our thinking as well as transform our actions.

JOURNEY OF PEASANTS

In this passage, as the Twelve are sent out, Jesus tells them to take a staff, wear their sandals and tunics, and go. They are to

73

dress lightly and go without a lot of fanfare or provisions. This might be different than what you or I consider taking when leaving on a journey. Compare the way we pack with the way Jesus instructed the Twelve to pack. Look at the lightness of their journey and the numbers of suitcases we often take.

• This can be a place to draw people in; those who travel frequently often keep a suitcase packed. They carry things so they can be as comfortable when traveling as they are when at home, which is in contrast to what Jesus seems to be doing here. Jesus seems to be indicating here that they are to take just a very little bit and go on their way.

• Peasants probably did not get to travel often, and they might have only one cloak and not have a second or a third. But also the one cloak represented some of the light travel that had been done by prophets such as Elijah or even John the Baptist.

They were to travel without provisions, showing that they were dependent on God to provide. They were visibly demonstrating that God was the source of their supply. They were to trust that in every city someone would welcome them and allow them to stay. They were sent to preach and to share a message; and in addition to their preaching, they healed and anointed.

This is awesome, for it seems to say to us that God will send us out in ways that might surprise us. God will send us with what appears to be the bare minimum and will expect us to do a work on his behalf. God will send us with no guarantees and will even expect us to be dependent on him during the trip. When the apostles travelled, they did not have an itinerary or schedule; they just went.

UNIQUE CLOTHES FOR UNIQUE LABOR

God's clothes are not necessarily the same as ours. God would send us clothed with the word, clothed with prayer, clothed with new values and attitudes. God will not always require us to take commentaries, curriculums, tracts, or other materials to do a work. It is not that those things are bad or not needed. They may just not be what is needed at this point. God wanted them to be able to meet the people where they were and really to understand the life they were living.

THE CLOTHES OF RECEIVING AND GIVING

We are clothed not just with knowledge, but also with a new attitude and understanding. They were to stay in the homes of those who had invited them and were to stay there and be dependent on those people's hospitality. In our society we hear the scripture, "It is more blessed to give than to receive" (Acts 20:35 KJV), and think that is the whole gospel. We have taken it to extremes and have failed to hear the entire gospel. In the gospel we are also taught that we need to be able to receive from others.

Considerations and Resources

• Consider a sermon series such as Clothed with Christ or Clothed for the Journey for use during the Lenten season. Other possibilities might be: Clothed with Boldness, Clothed for Transformation, Clothed for Prayer, or Clothed to Live in Community.

• Expand your time with children to include the entire congregation. Have several full-length bodies hanging around the sanctuary and lots of different shaped clothing made from construction paper or even stickers placed on index cards. Invite the congregation to think of their attitudes or values that they want to change during Lent and to place them on the body near their seats. (If you are a small- to mid-size congregation, you may be able to have these near the front and have people come forward as they do for an offering). This activity could happen one time, or it can be available throughout the Lenten season. On Easter or the following Sunday, have another time when people are able to go and take off the old as a symbol of the change that has occurred in their lives. (They would not have to find their own, but just take one off.)

• Think of Lent as the beginning of a journey for your congregation to reach out to the community. Today could be a time of commissioning outreach workers who will be visiting the homes of people in the community during the weeks of Lent.

My Thoughts and Ideas

_____

_____

_____

_____

_____

God Will Blow Your Mind!

Marsha Brown Woodward

Text

Isaiah 43:18-25; Habakkuk 1:5, 2:2-3

Theme

To impress upon the congregation that the best is yet to be.

Sermon Outline

MAKE SPACE FOR IMAGINATION

We are called to be a people who regularly "have their minds blown." We are a people who are, on a regular basis, supposed to be awed and amazed at what the God we serve is doing in the world. Our frequent conversation should be, "Look at God!" "Did you see what God just did?" "Awesome!" or even just a plain old, "Go, God!" Out of our mouths should come the phrases of praise that indicate we are aware of the movement of God in daily life. But to see this often takes imagination. God's new work often looks quite ordinary and unspectacular.

Some see a glass with water at the midway point as being half full; others see it as being half empty. This illustrates how, at times, we are blind to the possibility for newness. On the one hand, to see the glass as half empty is to see diminishment. "Diminishment vision" can lead to a spirit of fear and a need to hold tightly to the little that remains. On the other hand, to see the glass as half full is to have space for imagination and new possibilities. This space is the place where God can blow our minds.

God Is an Outrageous God

The text states that God is currently working. God says, "I am doing a new thing," not I *will* do or I am *thinking about* doing or *sometime in the future* I will do. God says, "I am *right now* doing a new thing." The Habakkuk text goes on to say that not only is it new, but if you could see it, your ears would tingle and your eyes would be amazed.

What does it take to amaze you? What could God do that would make your eyes grow wide and your ears tingle?

Celebrate What God Is Doing

• Look for the signs of change. How has God moved in this year, in the last five years, or even in the last twenty years? Think of the miracles in individual lives as well as in the life of the corporate community. What do they teach you about how God works?

• Where do you see the seeds of transformation, the beginnings of God's new work in your life?

• Confront your personal resistance to God's new thing. The cost of seeing the new might be personal and corporate change. What do you have to give up to accept the new? Look at the response by the leaders of his day to Jesus as he worked miracle after miracle in their midst. Often instead of rejoicing, they were angry. Could it be that it was hard to consider that they might have to change what they understood about God or God's law? We can be right in the midst of the new season and the new day and miss it because we are so locked into the old that we are willing to fight to keep things the way they are.

THERE ARE BLESSINGS WHEN GOD BLOWS OUR MINDS

- We learn new things about both God and ourselves.
- God will redefine the moment and redefine our lives.

Considerations and Resources

- Celebrate the power of change. How can you help people see the joyous possibilities in change? It might be fun to start by asking how many people would give up indoor plumbing for an outhouse, a stove and refrigerator for an icebox and an open fire, their automobiles for a horse and buggy, the telephone for no way to communicate with those in distant places except by telegram or letter. These changes were revolutionary at first, and yet we now see them as necessities.

- If you include a moment with children, have a clear glass with some water in it, and ask the children if it is half full or half empty.

- Interview older members. Are there people in the church or community who can remember the years of segregation and Jim Crow? Where are the restaurants and theatres that no one could envision African Americans entering? Are there hotels where African Americans could only be the maids and now serve as managers? Is there someone who could not vote and now is able to go to the polls? Paint a picture of a time when the future appeared limited, as a wilderness even, but which God transformed.

My Thoughts and Ideas

Prayer Plus

Marsha Brown Woodward

Text

John 17:1-26; Mark 9:14-29

Theme

To observe and celebrate the transformative power of prayer and fasting.

Sermon Outline

PRAYER AND JESUS

In John 17 we see the importance of prayer to Jesus. While on earth, Jesus stayed connected to God through prayer. In this chapter, he prays for himself, for those who believed through him, and for those who would yet believe. The groundwork is laid that prayer will be of value to those who believe in Jesus because it was of such importance to him.

SUPPORTING PRAYER WITH FASTING

Throughout Scripture there are many illustrations that we could use to show the importance of prayer. This passage in Mark not only highlights the importance of prayer, but also links prayer with other spiritual disciplines, in this case fasting. In the previous chapter, Jesus was transfigured; this account begins upon his return. Jesus heals the boy, but later, when they are alone, the disciples ask why they could not heal the boy. Jesus says, "This kind can come forth by nothing, but by prayer and fasting" (v. 29 KJV), as if to imply that though they had on the clothes of prayer, praying alone is not always enough. During Lent we often add fasting to our times of prayer. We intentionally sacrifice food or other activities in order to increase our time in prayer and to intercede for others.

FOCUSING COMMUNAL PRAYER AND FASTING

Where are the places in your community that represent the boy with seizures, the places that have long been in a condition that seems to defy healing? Would you and the congregation consider fasting and praying during this Lenten season on their behalf? Have you tried other solutions such as programs and grants and yet not found lasting solutions? Maybe healing will occur if you both pray and fast.

Considerations and Resources

• Fasting is a discipline that has lost its value and importance for many in the church. It is a time of sacrifice, often of food, but also of other things that are meaningful and important if they prevent us from spending time with God. Christian fasting draws us closer to God, and so it always includes time in reading and meditating on Scripture. Simply to go without food and without time of prayer and meditation is to diet. Consider an all-congregation fast. When I have done this, I have intentionally not done a food fast because some persons need to eat for health reasons. I have encouraged a fast from television, gossip, movies, video games, and other activities that people participate in and enjoy. I have also considered taking a time when a church activity would be held and asking everyone to spend that time in prayer.

• Have a day for fasting as a congregation. Consider Wednesday as the day for fasting, but ask each person to determine how much of the day he or she will join in the fast. In this instance, I might ask for a fast from foods because individuals can choose the time frame that will not jeopardize their overall health. Some might fast from midnight to midnight, from 6:00 A.M. to noon, from after breakfast until dinner, and so on. In this way everyone is fasting at some point during the day.

• Consider an all-church prayer vigil, lasting from several hours to several days. Consider having a variety of prayer times throughout the Lenten season. Become known as a congregation that takes prayer seriously. What would it look like if your congregation were known more for its prayer life than for your preaching or for the choirs? Lent may be the season to introduce the congregation to new forms of prayer. Consider placing a labyrinth in your fellowship hall for this six-week period.

• Invite the children into a time of prayer. Children are sometimes more open than adults to speak of things that concern them, and they may be willing to say what they would like the group to pray for that concerns them. If you are new to having a children's time, you could begin the list by saying sometimes schoolwork is hard and we want someone to pray for the children. Just remember to use illustrations that children experience.

My Thoughts and Ideas

_____

_____

_____

_____

Sometimes It Causes Me to Wonder

Marsha Brown Woodward

Text

Exodus 1:15-16, 22; Matthew 2:16-18

Theme

To reflect on the matter of "bad things" happening to "good people."

Sermon Outline

WHEN I THINK, I TREMBLE . . .

The ultimate sacrifice of the innocent we know is Jesus. The slaves of old caught the importance of remembering when they sang,

> Were you there when they crucified my Lord?
> Were you there when they crucified my Lord?
> Oh! Sometimes it causes me to tremble, tremble,
>   tremble.
> Were you there when they crucified my Lord?

I tremble because sometimes it is through the slaughter of the innocent that redemptive work occurs.

PHARAOHS AND HERODS

• Who are the babies today, the sons ordered to be killed, the daughters allowed to live? Push yourself to think outside the box and not just assume that the boy children have to be male and the girl children must be female. Think of male and female as a type. Who needs to be destroyed now because they would have power in the future? How are they killed? Could there be other deaths, even some literal deaths, occurring on a frequent basis? Who is weeping for the dead?

• Who are the Pharaohs and Herods, the kings "who knew not Joseph," the ones with little memory of the past, those who are fearful that someone can take their place? Fear is at least one of the ties that binds both Pharaoh and Herod. Can you identify other similar traits? Thinking of them as a type, who are the ones in those roles today?

IT'S BIGGER THAN AN INDIVIDUAL

• Evil is real. Systemic evil has a power that works through the Pharaohs and the Herods. Ephesians 6:12 says, "For our struggle is not against enemies of blood and flesh, but against the rulers, against the authorities, against the cosmic powers of this present darkness, against the spiritual forces of evil in the heavenly places." It is this mystery of the power of evil that sometimes discourages the people of God.

• At times, evil appears to be stronger. Why is it that people seem unable to come against the edict of the Pharaohs and the Herods? Midwives don't kill the male babies, but the individual parents apparently do. Joseph and Mary escape with Jesus, but many fathers and mothers see their male children die. And all we have is the record of great pain when the mothers weep. Why is it that evil, even seemingly, can intimidate the community of the faithful?

THEY, TOO, DIED FOR US

- We should give thanks for the countless numbers of African American women and of men, children, and those from other racial and ethnic groups who have worked for the freedom of African Americans through the sacrifice of their lives.

- The story of the four girls who were killed in Birmingham is told in the movie *4 Little Girls* and would help illustrate the tragedy of the slaughter of innocents.

- How can remembering their sacrifice empower us to work for change in our age? What is needed to dismantle systems of racism and "other isms"?

Considerations and Resources

- Before preaching this sermon, ask yourself what do you know about the congregation. Is this a congregation that already has some knowledge of systemic evil, or is evil a new concept for this congregation?

- View the movie, *4 Little Girls* and see both immediate responses and continued responses of the families to deal with this tragedy.

- Especially if you are preaching in a context where you will still be in relationship with the hearers (such as a pastor in a local congregation; a preacher for a revival, conference, or retreat; or where you will preach several sermons), be willing to allow people to experience pain and to resist the temptation to bring this sermon to the kind of conclusion that makes it appear that pain ends quickly. Part of the task of remembering is to live with the pain for a while.

- Are there actions that can be suggested for the hearers to take in response to the Pharaohs and Herods of today?

- If children are often in worship, consider how you may build a bridge for conversation with their parents or leaders after the sermon. Be sensitive when speaking of the killing of innocents, as this might be interpreted in their minds that they could literally be killed. Consider alerting leaders ahead of time so that they may be prepared.

• Adults also might benefit from times for reflection and discussion following the sermon. Consider a sermon feedback time.

• An unspoken question for many will be, "Where is God?" Be prepared with a response.

<u>My Thoughts and Ideas</u>

_____

_____

_____

_____

_____

A Love Letter Written in Blood

Teresa Fry Brown

Text
Luke 22:17-20

Theme
To celebrate God's deep affection for humanity.

Sermon Outline
FAVORITES

Do you have favorite poems, songs, or short pieces of prose that speak of love? My favorite one is Elizabeth Barrett Browning's "How Do I Love Thee?" Consider:
- societal images, beliefs, acts of love
- biblical understandings of love

FAREWELL DISCOURSE
- What does Jesus' last sermon contain?
- What is going on in Jerusalem at the time of the supper?
- Who are some of the named and unnamed characters in the passage?

PASSOVER MEAL (V. 14)
- What was served at the dinner, and what is the significance of each item?
- Imagine the table conversation. What words or phrases stand out for you?
- What does the way Jesus served the meal mean to you?
- Why should we remember the elements of the meal? Read verse 20.

A CONTEMPORARY LOVE LETTER

- If God wrote a letter to the church today, what would it say?
- How does blood signify love?

Considerations and Resources

- There are numerous website resources on the Seder meal. Think of ways that African American holiday cuisine signifies love.

- This sermon was written as a letter from Jesus to believers. Occasionally try an epistolary or letter sermon form. Thomas H. Troeger's *Ten Strategies for Preaching in a Multimedia Culture* (Nashville: Abingdon Press, 1996) should prove helpful.

- Read *Sankofa: Celebrations for the African American Church* by Grenaé Dudley and Carlyle Stewart (Cleveland, Ohio: United Church Press, 1997).

- Research beliefs and procedures for Communion services. Use new information to develop new words and new ways to observe Communion in your church.

My Thoughts and Ideas

_____

_____

_____

_____

_____

FIFTH SUNDAY IN LENT

Will You Let Jesus Wash Your Feet?

Marsha Brown Woodward

Text

John 13:1-17

Theme

It takes courage to risk being open with Christ.

Sermon Outline

FROM PETER'S PERSPECTIVE

Set the stage by retelling the story from the perspective of
Peter. Jesus and the Twelve have just eaten the meal we now call
the Last Supper. After dinner, Jesus gets up and takes a towel and
a basin of water and begins to wash feet. He moves around the
circle and has washed several feet, maybe those of everyone
except Peter. As Peter is watching, all kinds of thoughts go
through his head. Perhaps he wonders if he should be helping
Jesus. Maybe he wonders, "Is he going to wash my feet?"

PETER'S CHALLENGE

Peter was being confronted with all kinds of assumptions and
all kinds of ideas. This one act was turning Peter's world around,
maybe even upside down. Could he let Jesus wash his feet? He

wasn't afraid of being intimate with Jesus, for he had gotten used to eating with Jesus, and eating can be a sign of intimacy. You generally don't eat with just anybody. Foot washing was different. It was a place of vulnerability that Peter had not been before; it was a different level of their relationship. Here the leader was willing to serve the followers. It was blowing Peter's mind!

OUR CHALLENGE AND TRIUMPH

Will we let Jesus wash our feet? Are we willing to allow our leader, the Lord, to wash our feet? The easy, automatic response—since I am in church and know the right answer to give—is yes, the Lord can wash my feet. But stop and freeze the frame and invite the congregation to put themselves in the story. Imagine you are Peter, and walk in his place around the text. Does it feel different? Can you understand how awkward this made him and even makes you feel? It is so contrary to all we are taught, we are to serve the leader and not have the leader serve us. Even in groups that say there are no leaders, there tend to be unofficial leaders. Somehow whether official or unofficial, the leader is supposed to behave in a certain way, in a certain manner that does not include washing the feet of the followers. Will you be so open before Christ that nothing is kept back—that he sees your best sides and your not-so-good sides, that he gets all of you?

Even though we know that God knows all about us, we still in our humanness often try to protect ourselves, and even try to protect God from us. And to get this close, to allow Jesus to wash my feet is scary. Peter knew that the real story was that he was not deserving. Would we feel deserving? Jesus washed feet so they and we would understand grace. The great triumph and joy is that it's not about what we deserve, but what God offers— just because. The triumph continues as we go and wash the feet of another.

Considerations and Resources

• This sermon could be ended in a variety of ways. A traditional way would be to have a service of foot washing. Leaders of the congregation could gather and take a towel and a basin and go into the congregation and wash the feet of those gathered. There are many variations on this, from having people come forward and the officers wash their feet, to having people come forward to place their hands over a bowl and have water poured over their hands as a symbol of having their feet washed. This is also good practice for those who are unable to take their shoes off for physical reasons, or for those who have amputated limbs or are in a cast.

• Conclude the sermon by inviting the congregation to continue reflecting on the message at a later time. Encourage them to do a self-guided meditation:

> *Find a place where you can be alone. Read or reflect on this passage and then get still. Be at the table with Jesus, laughing, talking, and enjoying the meal. See Jesus get up; see Jesus pick up a bowl and begin to wash feet.*
>
> *Now see Jesus in front of you, see him kneel down, feel his eyes as they lock into your eyes, feel him reaching to take off your sandals. Stay in that moment; don't run from it or rush it; allow Jesus to wash your feet.*
>
> *As he washes your feet, believe that all the things you are trying to keep hidden from the world are being washed away—all the secrets, the hurts, the pains—things that he already knows about, you no longer have to keep from him. See how free you feel, how new, how strengthened.*
>
> *Slowly come back to the space where you are and take a few minutes to thank God for what you experienced.*

• Children might not think it such an odd thing that Jesus is washing their feet, because they are used to adults washing them, no matter how dirty they might be. So the challenge may be to ask them if there is someone they can be kind to, but who doesn't expect them to be kind.

• While this sermon could be used at any point during the Lenten season, it would be especially appropriate on Maundy, or Holy, Thursday. Consider a live sermon, in which you act out the text. Have a table set up, with individuals reclining at the table and not objecting as Jesus washes their feet. Peter could develop his role even more to include part of the dialogue of the sermon.

My Thoughts and Ideas

_____

_____

_____

_____

_____

The Bitter and the Better in All of Us

Kirk Byron Jones

Text

Matthew 26:47-49; 27:3-5

Theme

To celebrate grace over dread and sin.

Sermon Outline

THE BITTER

Is there any name so utterly unacceptable as the name *Judas?*
History offers some suggestions: Jezebel (slayer of prophets),
Brutus (assassin of Caesar), Benedict Arnold (betrayer of the
American cause), and Hitler (murderer of innocent millions).
These are the infamous names of history, names that have
become curse words, and words we use to identify the vile and
foul among us. When you refer to someone as a "Jezebel" or
"Brutus" or "Benedict Arnold" or "Judas," you are not just calling
that person out-of-name, but you are calling them out of all that
is holy, just, and good.

There is *bitter* in us all. If the Bible is clear about the drawbacks
and imperfections of Judas, it is even clearer about the drawbacks
and imperfections of us all. See Isaiah 53:6, Luke 18:19, and
Romans 7:19.

THE BETTER

There is *better* in us all. We are made, David says, "a little lower
than God, and [are] crowned . . . with glory and honor" (Psalm 8:5).

We are the made in the image of God. There is better in our bitter. Even Judas had better. Only Matthew picks it up; Judas said he was sorry.

In the spirit of the one Judas betrayed, I'm led to speculate that perhaps the biggest mistake Judas made that night was not what he did, but what he didn't do. Perhaps his biggest mistake was not that he turned Jesus over, but that he didn't turn himself over to Jesus, the personification of God's unconditional love and grace.

Considerations and Resources

• View the film *Imitation of Life*. Feel the pain of a daughter's remorse and grief.

• Read Psalm 32:5. How does this text support the conclusion of this sermon?

• Reflect on the history and lyrics of the song "Amazing Grace."

• Though you may disagree with the content, the recent scholarship on the Gospel of Judas should not be ignored. Read "The Judas Gospel" by Andrew Cockburn (*National Geographic* vol. 209, no. 5 [May 2006]).

My Thoughts and Ideas

APRIL

ARTICLES

Easter Preaching: Can We Handle the Resurrection?

Kirk Byron Jones

I. Who Can Handle Resurrection Properly?

As I began to focus on what I might contribute to our gathering on the theme "Preaching and the Resurrection," I had a flashback. My mind went back to a novel I read some years ago, *Lazarus*, by Alain Absire (San Diego: Harcourt Brace Jovanovich, 1988). It is an imagined account of what happened to Lazarus once he was revived from the dead. In the middle of the song "Mary Don't You Weep, Martha Don't You Mourn," Aretha Franklin tells the story of the resurrection of Lazarus. According to the gospel of Aretha, Lazarus "got up walking like a natural man." Absire sees it differently. The residue of the resurrection for Lazarus is an unnaturalness that has him, at times, longing to be dead again. Absire writes:

> Lazarus, who had spent whole days sleeping when he first returned from the grave, now could not sleep at all. He tossed and turned from the first hour of the night until the last. He threw away his pillows and tried lying flat, then retrieved them and put them under his neck. Suddenly cold, he wrapped himself in the blanket; then just as suddenly he was hot and threw it off again. Although he often moved close to Susannah [his wife], as she lay beside him, he would move away again almost at once, for fear of offending her, repelling her by his smell or by the coldness of his skin. Whatever he did, whatever position he tried, he stayed awake, and was preyed upon by melancholy thoughts . . .
>
> One night, unable to bear lying awake, he rose, wrapped himself in his cloak, and went up to the roof. There, looking out into the darkness, he recalled how he used to love these cold nights of Passover. He had breathed in the smells of warm

earth and wild plants; had listened to the thousands of faint sounds quickening the enormous silence; had gazed at the multitude of stars dotting the blue-black sky and shedding a mist of light over the hills. Now, he could not smell the spring or hear its rustlings . . .

Imprisoned in an impenetrable fog, all he could do was shiver from the cold.

Some pages later, Absire's Lazarus leaves this lament with Mary, the mother of Jesus, "He would have done better to leave me in the tomb."

Lazarus is not the same. Who he is, whoever and whatever that is, is a far cry from who he used to be. He wants a ticket back to death. And this time he wants to make sure that it is stamped "one way." Lazarus cannot handle resurrection. Who can?

II. Who Can Handle Resurrection Homiletically?

You and I know we have our hands—not to mention our minds, hearts, and nerves—full just handling preaching. And if legendary, tenured pulpiters are telling the truth, the burden of preaching does not lighten with years.

Caesar Clark, the great evangelist, once referred to his efforts as "embarrassed stammering."

Embarrassed stammering, yes. But something within and without, time and time again, anoints our suspect communication, making it matter. So Clark, you, and I keep getting back up there. If preaching, in general, is embarrassed stammering, preaching resurrection from the dead is even more so, especially in our world.

In our world of technological mastery and wizardry, of unprecedented scientific breakthroughs, how dare we repeat reports over two thousand years old of a man who raised the dead and who was himself raised from the dead. Can we preach anything more embarrassing and downright foolish than that?

And something in addition to absurdity may contribute to resurrection's deterioration in the minds of many: the minimization of its novelty. How unique is resurrection in a world no longer impressed by the supposition or realization of human cloning? We more easily, less queasily, imagine fabricating new life and refurbishing old life. In Boston, the death of baseball great Ted Williams was shrouded by a family feud over whether or not to freeze his remains for possible revival (resurrection) in the future. In the movie *Solaris*, people not only come back from the dead, but also keep coming back from the dead. Resurrections of the same individuals occur over and over again.

For lo these many centuries, the main barrier to resurrection reality has been its believability. It was for those who first heard it, and has been for many since, too incredible to believe. Now, for the first time, there is a new barrier on the horizon that may rival the old one: Christian resurrection is not incredible enough. Can we handle that? How can we handle that?

III. Less Is More

I believe we will have a better go of handling the Resurrection homiletically in our world if we practice verbal and literary restraint.

Less is more.

Less is more when it comes to our words about resurrection. We stand a better chance of preaching about resurrection by using fewer but finer words because our world suffers, as someone has put it, from "verbal intoxication."

We stand a better chance of preaching about resurrection by using fewer but finer words because Barbara Brown Taylor is right when she says in her book, *When God Is Silent*, "Christianity is an overly talkative religion" ([Cambridge, Mass.: Cowley Publications, 1998], 74). Fewer, finer words and more silence are what we need.

The poets are our beacon lights. Especially poets such as Gillian Conoley, who said in a recent interview: "I find myself very attracted to poetry that has a lot of white space lately. I find that sort of work restful. Not to have a page covered with words is somehow more inviting. I want to go into that world" ("Where

Silence Sends Word," interview with Gillian Conoley, by Kevin Larimer, *Poets & Writers Magazine*, Jan/Feb 2001, 32).

To have a sermon on resurrection, or any sermon for that matter, not covered and plastered with words is more inviting. This matter transcends sermonizing in the mind of the sage Abraham Joshua Heschel: "The strength of faith (Heschel said) is in silence, and in words that hibernate and wait. Uttered faith must come out as surplus of silence, as the fruit of lived faith, of enduring intimacy" (Abraham Joshua Heschel, *Moral Grandeur and Spiritual Audacity: Essays*, ed. Susannah Heschel [New York: Farrar, Straus & Giroux, 1996], 264).

Less is more in our preaching in regard to words, our articulations about resurrection, and our overall apprehension of resurrection. I am more and more put off by any preaching (my own and yours) that betrays an over-apprehension of the gospel:

• preaching that is too sure of itself
• preaching that smacks of a mastery of divinity
• preaching that is fully stocked with all of the right answers

Awhile back I was flying into Boston and experienced what is referred to in aviation lingo as an "aborted landing." The landing had been announced, and we all had gone through the procedure of putting our trays back into place, bringing up our seats—you know the drill. The plane had even started its descent downward, and suddenly back up we went. Our arrival, due to fog, I later learned, was delayed. Although such a thing may not be desired in air travel, it ought to be our desire in our travels about the gospel; we ought never give the faintest evidence of having arrived. To do this is to empty the gospel of its mystery, its wonder, its awe, its power.

Preaching that is less sure of itself, but no less faithful, will not insist on a head-on, head-only engagement with the gospel. The kind of preaching I am trying to see more clearly and do more confidently teases and suggests more than it pronounces. It steps more gingerly, softly, and at times secretly. It is not ashamed of its budding friendship with imagination. It has been altogether persuaded by Rainer Maria Rilke's plea to "love the questions themselves." It is more comfortable with leaving the sermon as open at the end as it was at the beginning.

IV. Handled by Resurrection

I have suggested that we can handle resurrection homiletically as we cease using all those words and resist being all too sure. There is something else. In order to handle resurrection, we must be handled by resurrection. Peter Gomes preached one of the most fascinating and moving sermons on the Resurrection I have ever heard.

When he was done I made my way around the side of the church to be one of the first ones to greet him as he exited. I embraced him and whispered, "That's one of those sermons that makes me glad that I am a preacher."

In his sermon, he proposed that the Resurrection was a continuing event that involves everyone who dares be involved with it. Said Gomes, "Easter is not just about Jesus, it's about you. Jesus has already claimed his new life. What about you? Easter is not just about the past, it's about the future. Your best days are ahead of you. The proof of the Resurrection is in your hands and in your life."

Handling the Resurrection is challenging; being handled by the Resurrection is even more challenging. In Absire's novel, Lazarus's problem was not being raised, but being raised different. He was not the same person. Christian resurrection is about not just coming back to life, but coming back to life different. We don't do different well. In social relations, all too often we interpret different as deficient. In our own minds, we so despise the different that it has been estimated that 90 percent of the thoughts anyone thinks on any given day are the same as those of the day before.

Being handled by the Resurrection means constantly challenging our fear of the unknown and, even more, according to Anthony De Mello, constantly challenging our fear "of the loss of the known."

Being handled by the Resurrection means learning to relax in the experience of new life. May we enter with God into the work of spiritually and emotionally modulating, changing, and recomposing our lives. May we rise and cheer such resurrections, now and forever. Amen.

The Art, the Agony, and the Amazement of Preaching

Cedric Kirkland Harris

For more than twenty-two years, I have been trying to preach, trying to master the art, trying to overcome the agony, trying to understand the amazement. So then, this essay is an admission, a confession of my past and present stammerings and possible fate. My hope is that this confession will be good for my soul, that I will be encouraged to keep on trying, as I must, although I may never truly preach.

In the spring of 1981, as I was preparing to graduate and was packing up my belongings to leave the Hill (Andover Newton), I came across an old blue shoebox stuffed with sermons dated from 1973 through 1978, the five years of my novitiate service at Bethel Baptist Church in Orange, New Jersey. The shoebox included my trial sermon (an excruciating narrative detailing the life of Samson and all four chapters of Judges 13–16) preached at Bethel Baptist Church. In that old blue shoebox I rediscovered youth revival sermons; a sermon preached to the Lott Carey Foreign Mission Convention; four or five eulogies; and twenty-five or thirty other sermons preached at Bethel and at our sister churches. Although I did not have the time (we never do when we are packing to leave), I took the time to read them all, recalling the experiences, seeing the faces, feeling the rhythms of preaching, singing, praying, and worshiping in the African American church. The sermons in that old blue shoebox provided a living recollection of my early years of ministry and attempts at sacred rhetoric.

But the deception of my agonizing pride was too great for me to endure and accept. So when I had finished reading, reminiscing, and reaping my past, I took that old blue shoebox and its remains outside and laid it to rest, carefully placing that makeshift coffin underneath garbage in the garbage bin behind

Farwell Hall. No one, I thought to myself, would ever have the opportunity to do a critical review of the homiletical form and theological content of my sermons or of me. No one would ever know what I knew: that I had failed at the art and flunked in the act of preaching. For then, in 1981, after a few years of theological education, a few courses in homiletics, and a few more sermons under my belt, I knew better and was a better preacher, and it would not be fair (after a stellar preaching career) for anyone to find this old blue shoebox when I'm gone and say, "Oh, but look at what he was preaching back then!"

So, in the spring of 1981, I buried that old blue shoebox and part of myself in a garbage bin behind Farwell Hall. I thought that I had buried, once and for all, all my agony, all of my futile attempts of preaching. But now, fourteen years after its burial, I have a greater respect for the power of resurrection, for now every week for preaching is Holy Week. Every weekend is a Golgotha experience. And every Sunday morning, that old blue shoebox is raised from the dead!

Several months ago, I read Dr. Samuel Proctor's *The Certain Sound of the Trumpet: Crafting a Sermon of Authority* (Valley Forge, Pa.: Judson Press, 1994) and wrote to him expressing gratitude for helping me understand and clarify what I was doing in the introductions of my sermons. My wife, Linda, had often commented that my introductions tended to be long and tough to follow. Of course, I could not hear her criticisms. We have a standing rule, a gag rule, that we do not offer any form of constructive criticism about each other's sermons. If one does well, say you enjoyed it. If not, then say nothing. Isn't this how our parishioners respond? Unknowingly, in my introductions I was engaged in a conceptual dialectic between the *kerygma* of Jesus as the major thesis over against the antithesis of our lived realities. Dr. Proctor's suggestions offered me this insight and helped me sharpen the art of my preaching by structuring my introductions in such a way that I state the dialectical tensions and make connections to the experiences of my listeners. You see, I have this thing about being clear as well as honest with the text and yet recognizing the strenuous realities of our lives. And I want to "say it" well. Saying it well—preaching in the African American tradition—is an art. As one member of Bank Street Church will tell me on occasion, "If I want to hear a lecture, I'll go over to Norfolk State University. I come to church to hear good preaching!" Although he has never preached, he and everyone else at Bank Street Church and your church know what the art of preaching sounds like and feels like. They know "the certain sound of the trumpet."

But do they know about the agony of preaching? Do they know about old blue shoeboxes? Do our parishioners know anything about the preacher's agonizing search for ultimate meaning; how we must dare to speak what we know will be at times painful to hear? Do they know anything about the question, "What's redemptive in this story; what can we possibly celebrate with integrity?" Do they know anything about the lies being preached in the name of God and Jesus Christ versus the prophetic proclamation of love, truth, and justice? Do they know the difference between being fooled and the foolishness of the gospel? Yes, I think that most of them do know something of our agony. They know something about that old blue shoebox and agonizing memories thought to have been buried and tossed away. They know and feel the agony of authentic preaching because they have known and felt the agonies in their own lives. In a commencement sermon addressed to the 1995 graduating class at the Interdenominational Theological Center in Atlanta, Dr. Renita Weems said, "People may not know about homiletics nor how to spell it, but they do know a lie when they hear one!"

In the spring of 1981, I failed to realize the amazing power and grace of what was in that old blue shoebox. I thought it was a coffin when, in fact, it was the Ark of the Covenant. For despite all of my failed attempts at mastering this fine art; despite those Sundays when after preaching my best I sometimes feel that I have flunked; despite the embarrassment of my stammering tongue; despite the risk of speaking the truth in love rather than the impossible option of saying nothing at all; despite and in light of what the late Dr. Gene Bartlett called the "audacity of preaching"; despite knowing the best that I can say is simply what Jesus has already said, knowing in my head and in my heart that to our experiences and our questions of human suffering and mental anguish I can only say, "just hold on and be faithful to the end"; despite what I don't know about the art of preaching or how preaching works; despite the agony that I feel week after week, Sunday after Sunday; despite it all, I have discovered the amazing power in the resurrected remains of old blue shoeboxes! For in the weakness, Christ has been strong. In the decay and ashes of my tangled and mixed up words, somehow the Word of God lives.

I am amazed on those Sundays when, in the Baptist tradition, I open the doors of the church, and someone makes a decision to welcome Christ into his or her life and walks down the aisle of Bank Street Church. I am amazed when, after the service, a congregant comes up to me and says, "Pastor, you were talking to me this morning. Thank you so much." I am absolutely amazed when that congregant's mother comes up to me and says, "Now, Reverend, when I die, I want you to preach my funeral, so don't you plan on going anywhere." I am amazed when a married couple, both of whom happen to be doctors, send me a note expressing their gratitude for my preaching and pastoral leadership and tell me not to get discouraged. Of course, I am amazed when a four-year-old says to me, "You sound like God when you preach!" I am amazed that someone—no, more than one, if not everyone—is listening to the preacher for a word from the Lord that will give guidance for his or her life; a word of affirmation from the Almighty; a hint of hope from heaven; a verbal caress that will bring comfort; a verdict of justice from the Court of God's Temple that assures the ultimate triumph of good over evil; a word from the preacher that will review and give meaning to all of what happened during the last week and offer a forecast of impossible possibilities for the week to come.

Almost every Sunday, a church member will come up to me and say, "Well, Reverend, you're still batting a 1,000!" Immediately, my feelings about the art and the agony and the amazement are stirred up. So I respond to his affirmation by saying, "You know, if I were a baseball player and hit .500, I would be the highest paid athlete in the world and be guaranteed a place in baseball's Hall of Fame, but as a preacher, I would be a total failure!"

This confession has been good for my soul. I realize that I was wrong to bury that old blue shoebox. We thank God for the resurrection of old blue shoeboxes.

April

APRIL

SERMON OUTLINES

Week One

PALM/PASSION SUNDAY

Sanctified Tension

Kirk Byron Jones

Text

Luke 22:23

Theme

To understand that tension is a vital component of healthy spiritual growth.

Sermon Outline

THE LAST SUPPER

How many different paintings of the Last Supper are there in existence? How many different sketches or other works of art have as their central focus the last meal Jesus has with the disciples before he marches to Calvary? How many capture the "tension" of the moment?

WHAT IS TENSION?

The dictionary definition of tension:
• The act of straining or stretching, the condition of being strained or stretched
• A state of mental unrest, often with signs of bodily stress

- A state of latent (present but not visible) hostility or opposition
  - Voltage

VIOLENT TENSION

It is understandable why something deep down inside of us resists and rejects this tension created by abuse and murder. This is violent tension.

SANCTIFIED TENSION

But there is another kind of tension we can't afford to resist and reject (or leave out of the picture), a tension Martin Luther King Jr. called "a type of constructive nonviolent tension that is necessary for growth" (from "Letter from Birmingham City Jail," in *A Testament of Hope: The Essential Writings and Speeches of Martin Luther King, Jr.*, ed. James M. Washington [San Francisco: HarperSanFrancisco, 1991], 291). One example of this kind of tension is the tension that arises when different people come together with different views on things, or when different people come together, period. This tension is constructive tension, sanctified tension that invites our traveling through it, not around it, or avoiding it altogether. The traveling-through sanctified tension demands sanctified ways of relating with one another, holy modes of interpersonal transportation, including the following: honesty, openness, understanding, grace, and commitment.

Contributions and Resources

- Study the word *tension*.
- Discern between creative and destructive forms of tension. Converse with others, and secure examples and illustrations for this sermon.
- Why might we fear tension?

My Thoughts and Ideas

_____

_____

_____

_____

_____

Facing Our Jerusalems

Kirk Byron Jones

Text

Matthew 21:6-13

Theme

To stir up courageous faith amid adversity.

Sermon Outline

UNSCHEDULED PARADES

- Parades happen in New Orleans year-round, not just during Mardi Gras season.
- Jesus had entered Jerusalem before, many times, but never before with such pomp, pageantry, and glitz. His arrival was an unscheduled parade of sorts.
- Just as surprising and unscheduled is Jesus' hand in it all. Though he is comfortable enough in crowds in his ministry, more than a few times, his goal was to escape the crowd to squash the notoriety. He's riding with the masses toward the masses.
- It's not just that he is riding, but *how* he is riding. Seemingly, he is role-playing an ancient prophecy in Zechariah 9:9: "Your king comes to you; / triumphant and victorious is he, / humble and riding on a donkey, / on a colt, the foal of a donkey." Jesus knows that his riding is going to create a stir amongst people hungry for a liberator from the domination and oppression of Rome, thirsty for the restoration of Israel and Jerusalem.

OUR JERUSALEMS

We could spend time thinking more about what the ride that day meant for Jesus, what it meant for those in the crowd. For the moments of this sermon, let us focus on what it means to face our Jerusalems. First and foremost, Jerusalem is a geographical location in the Middle East of about forty-three square miles, a holy city to Jews, Christians, and Muslims, containing sites sacred to all three religions. Consider Jerusalem as representative of significant realities in life that we all do well to face, to ride toward and not run away from.

- We face our Jerusalems when we face our callings in life.
- Hearing and honoring our calls in life is our life's work.
- What is God calling you to do?
- We face our callings when we face trials.
- Jerusalem may be any adversity.
- The greater the challenge, the greater the growth.

GOD RIDES WITH US THROUGH IT ALL

In the song "Through It All," Andraé Crouch says that he has "learned to trust in Jesus" and has "learned to trust in God."

Considerations and Resources

- In *Let Your Life Speak: Listening for the Voice of Vocation*, Parker Palmer offers: "Vocation is rooted in the Latin for 'voice.' Vocation does not mean a goal that I pursue. It means a calling that I hear. Before I can tell my life what I want to do with it, I must listen to my life telling me who I am" (San Francisco: Jossey-Bass, 2000).
- Ask the congregation, "Do you know the richest place in the world?" They will be surprised when you give as an answer, "The graveyard—besting oil fields and all the riches that can be found anywhere else—the place where unused callings, gifts, and dreams are buried."
- Regularly consult newspapers, periodicals, and books for stories of triumph over tragedy.
- Attend to your own triumphs over tragedy. Resist overly referring to yourself in preaching, but "testify" from your own experience when you feel strongly led to do so.

<u>My Thoughts and Ideas</u>

_____

_____

_____

_____

_____

Week Two

Resurrection Surrender

Kirk Byron Jones

Text

Luke 24:1-5

Theme

To challenge people to experience the resurrection surrender.

Sermon Outline

BOWING

Most of us don't usually bow when we greet someone. In some cultures, we would bow to others as a common courtesy. We usually bow our heads when we are asked to bless our food or pray in church. At other times when we pray, we bow not just our heads, but our bodies. I still carry in my heart an image of my father bowing on his knees in prayer. Groomsmen bow to bridesmaids as part of the marriage ceremony. Adult entertainers may not do it as much, but children who have performed, no matter how well or poorly, are still encouraged to "take a bow" as a way of receiving gratitude from the audience.

On this Resurrection Sunday, the day we celebrate the greatest *rising up* in history, there is a *bowing down* that we should celebrate and emulate. Mary Magdalene, Mary, the mother of James, and Salome make their way to the tomb at daybreak and

115

find that the carefully wrapped corpse is missing. The biblical chronicle doesn't say, "They were terrified and turned away" or "They were terrified and ran away" or "They were terrified and fainted." The record reads: "They were terrified and *bowed* their faces to the ground."

KINDS OF BOWING
Sunkupto

The Greek word for bowed, *sunkupto*, might have been used, but it is not. *Sunkupto* means to bow together with an infirmity or some other reality causing the bowing. It is the word used in reference to the woman who is bowed down, crippled with an infirmity, for eighteen years in Luke 13:11. But *sunkupto*, "to bow with," is not the word used.

Sunkampto

The word *sunkampto* might have been used, but it is not. This is the kind of bowing that we are *made* to do, "forced bowing." The text says that two men are in the tomb as well "in dazzling clothes." For all the women knew, in the fog of the morning and the fear of the moment, these men might have been mistaken for Roman soldiers. If this was the case, the women may have been made to bow out of forced respect for oppressive power. Being made to bow is a form of human diminishment and shrinking.

• No one is born to live, bowed in this way. No one should remain stuck in the downward posture of low self-esteem.

• We were all born to soar.

Kampto

The word *kampto* might have been used, but it is not. This is the bowing we do out of religious respect or adoration.

• *Kampto* certainly would have been appropriate given where they were.

• *Kampto* bowing can happen anywhere, at any time.

• The great fourteenth-century poet Rumi reminds us, "There are hundreds of ways to kneel and kiss the ground."

THE BOW OF SURRENDER—KLINO

The word used for their bowing before the Resurrection is *klino*, the same one used in John 19:30 of Jesus dying on the cross, "Then he bowed his head and gave up his spirit." Jesus bowed: Jesus put his head in a position of rest and peaceful surrender.

The women bowed: "Lord, we don't know what's going on here, and the truth is we are afraid. What has happened is more than we can stand, so we bow. We rest our fears and all that we are on you."

I hear the songwriter singing,

> I surrender all,
> I surrender all,
> All to thee, my blessed Savior,
> I surrender all.
>
> (J. W. Van Deventer, 1896)

CAN WE BOW BEFORE THE RESURRECTION?

Can we rest our fears about death—and life—in the Resurrection? Can we bow? Can we surrender our worries in the empty tomb? Can we bow? Can we trust what Alice Walker refers to as the true wine of astonishment: We are not over when we think we are. Can we bow? Can we release our dread because Jesus is not dead? He is alive! Can we bow before the Resurrection?

Can we bow into the Resurrection? Jesus claimed his new life; can you claim yours?

Considerations and Resources

• *Seeing Jazz: Artists and Writers on Jazz* (San Francisco: Chronicle Books, 1997) is an amazing collection of pictures, prose, and poetry. On page 12 of this text, you will see a picture taken by Milt Hinton in 1941. Hinton captured three jazz musicians, Cozy Cole, Danny Barker, and Chad Collins, in a posture of greeting one another. In this perfectly proportioned, black-and-white picture taken in New Orleans, the three men are tipping their hats and bowing to one another. Just one look at the photograph and it is obvious that the subjects are doing more than merely welcoming one another. They are—in a segregated society that often refused to recognize their humanity—*honoring* one another. Their bowing was *kampto* bowing, holy and sacred bowing.

• *Tashi deley* is a Tibetan phrase that means "I honor the greatness in you. I honor the place in you where lives your courage, honor, love, hope, and dreams." What does surrendering mean to you? What are negative understandings associated with surrendering?

• What is the relationship between healthy self-esteem and spiritual surrendering?

My Thoughts and Ideas

Which Crowd Were You In?

Text

Matthew 21:1-10, 45-46; 27:15-17, 20-22

Theme

To experience the last week of Jesus' life in a new way.

Sermon Outline

CROWDS

Crowds can be powerful and crowds can be dangerous. How we act in a crowd often surprises us. Parents often try to teach their children to think for themselves, so that if they find themselves in the midst of a crowd at school, they will not automatically do what the majority is doing. Youth are encouraged to think for themselves, so that when they are at a party and someone starts to use alcohol or drugs, they will make a better choice. But still even as adults, if we are not careful, we discover that time and time again, we can pick up the mentality and the mind-set of the crowd.

• Give examples of how this might manifest itself in both small ways—such as being in a line and everyone else is grumbling and you start grumbling as well—to large ways—such as being with a group and suddenly they start breaking windows and throwing rocks and you find yourself joining in.

• In that final week, Jesus faced three crowds: the Palm Sunday crowd, the crowd during the week that gathers as he is teaching and healing, and the crowd before Pilate that yells "Crucify him." Find yourself in each of the crowds.

THE THREE CROWDS
The Crowd of Welcome

The first crowd was seen as Jesus approaches Jerusalem. Jesus set his face to go to Jerusalem; he had been on a direct path that led to this place and now he was getting close. Matthew's Gospel says he was at Bethpage (on the Mount of Olives), which is just a couple of miles outside the city. Jesus sent two of the disciples (not necessarily one of the Twelve) into town and told them to borrow a colt and a donkey. And they did. When they returned, they placed their cloaks on the animals and Jesus sat on them. A crowd had been following as well, and the crowd began to place their cloaks on the road. Others began to cry out, "Hosanna to the Son of David! Blessed is the one who comes in the name of the Lord! Hosanna in the highest heaven!" (21:9).

The Crowd of Listening

The second crowd was the one that we saw on the next day when Jesus returned to teach. He taught, and a crowd gathered and listened intently. This crowd had many of those who had followed along the way, those who had heralded his entrance into the city, now joined by others. There were the ones in the temple courts who had faintly heard of this teacher and now had a chance to hear him directly; there were some bystanders who just happened to be there; there were some soldiers representing the government; there were some upset businesspeople trying to see who this man was who had overturned their tables the day before. They were all there in the crowd, with many different motivations; but from the outside, no one could see who was who; it was just a crowd. All week this crowd followed Jesus around, and I believe the crowd kept growing and became more and more and more diverse.

You can understand this, for similar things happen today when something is new or someone is in the news. The more media attention that person gets, the larger the crowds that follow him or her. Granted, in our day it is usually not teachers, but you can imagine what it would be like. And the numbers of the crowds continue to swell. Many come because they are seeing the miracles; others because they are hearing the teaching; but others because they are upset and are looking for ways to trap Jesus, to hear him say the wrong thing.

The Crowd of Fear

There was a third crowd that week. Although this crowd included many of the same people, there was a change. The crowd had become disappointed and sad. Fear became a motivator more than faith and hope, and this crowd was fearful.

WHICH CROWD WERE WE IN?

It is easy to see ourselves in the Sunday crowd, cheering Jesus, but we also need to see where we would have been on Friday. Some of us will even have to admit that we were not in the crowd on Sunday or during the week or on Friday. We managed to have an excuse for not being there at all. Others would say they were there at the beginning, but as the mood of the crowd changed, it was safer to stay at home. It was not our business and we have enough problems to deal with without taking on the issues of Jesus. Still others would have stayed because they were convinced that something dramatic would occur and they wanted to be in on the action.

What does it mean for us? All of us can deny Jesus; all of us are capable of betraying him. All of us can sell him out. All of us can turn tail and run. In our humanness, we are not very strong. When we are able to be honest with ourselves, we can be honest with him. When we realize that we could be the one yelling, "Crucify him," then it can help us in understanding why we need to seek mercy and forgiveness.

Easter service again is a crowd, but a transformed crowd that remembers that they have journeyed during the past week from joy to sorrow in a way that enables them to experience joy in a new way.

Remembering Jesus' experience with crowds will give us strength to face the crowds that we will meet on our journeys of faith.

Considerations and Resources

• Carry the theme throughout the week leading up to Easter. Hold a midweek service, with the objective of building toward Sunday's worship joy. As you move toward Thursday and Friday, focus on the changing mood of the crowd, the fear and anxiety, the questions being raised by many. Good Friday service might end with the questions in the hearts of many and the crowd moving underground. Consider an Easter vigil on Saturday. Let this be a time to stay in the pain that the first followers experienced. Now welcome the Resurrection—the women coming with the great news that Jesus is risen—with an early morning service. Consider acting out the crowd scenes. You may also consider using a video clip from the movie *Miracle Maker*, which is animated but very good for children and adults.

• Continue your Lenten focus during the season of Eastertide (from Easter to Pentecost). If Lent is a time to learn more about Jesus and our relationship to him, then the journey from Easter to Pentecost can be a time of learning how we live for him. The Lenten questions are of an inward nature, and the questions leading toward Pentecost help us focus on our outward responsibilities.

My Thoughts and Ideas

_____

_____

_____

_____

_____

Week Three

Post-Easter Blues or Resurrection Joy?

Cheryl Kirk-Duggan

Text

John 20

Theme

To celebrate Easter as opportunity for daily resurrection joy.

Sermon Outline

SOMETIMES IN THE MIDST OF THE EVENTS, WE FORGET WHY WE CELEBRATE

- Remember the story of the passion and Resurrection?
- What did you do Easter Sunday afternoon and each day since?
- Does Easter really make a difference?
- The disciples were fearful; the women had been silent witnesses.
- When they see Jesus again, they rejoice, and they are changed forever.

TO DO THE WORK, WE NEED THE POWER

- When we need the work of a professional, we want the most experienced. Why?

- In John's Gospel, Jesus anoints the disciples with the Holy Spirit. Their living experience is transformed.
- Now the disciples are fully equipped to do the work, to teach, preach, and be vessels for healing.
- Jesus also cautions the disciples to be open for forgiveness and not to hold grudges.
- Have you received the power? Are you holding grudges? Who do you need to forgive?

DOUBTING IS THE OTHER SIDE OF FAITH

- Thomas listened but could not believe; Thomas had post-Easter blues.
- Thomas was honest. Are we being honest today in our lives?
- Jesus had room for Thomas's doubt and never ridiculed or put him down.
- Jesus awaits our own doubt and our faith.
- You can experience daily resurrection joy through faith amid doubt.

Considerations and Resources

- Consider consulting with a counselor about the importance of owning and honoring all of our emotions, including our fears and doubts.
- Read *Feel the Fear and Do It Anyway* by Susan Jeffers (New York: MJF Books).
- Before preaching that doubting is the other side of faith, test this contention with members of your congregation or complete strangers. Allow responses to generate additional sermon ideas and questions.
- Are there "hidden blessings in doubt"? Does doubt have to prevent daily joy?
- How may doubt help grow faith?
- Must we all go through "seasons" of doubt in our lives? Remember some of your "doubting seasons." What did they teach you?

My Thoughts and Ideas

_____

_____

_____

_____

_____

Do You Love Me?

Kirk Byron Jones

Text

John 21:15-17

Theme

To observe the redemptive power of healing forgiveness.

Sermon Outline

FRESH STARTS

Successful head football coach Bill Parcells once issued t-shirts to his coaches and players during training camp with a simple message printed on the back: START OVER. He was trying to warn the rising team of the east that they couldn't win this year's games on last year's success; they would have to *start over*.

In the wake and wonder of the Resurrection, Jesus and Simon, son of John, are starting over. Their new start soars on the wings of a question asked by Jesus: "Do you love me?"

PETER'S RELEASE, AND OURS

Ever since the night before the crucifixion, Peter had been carrying a burden around that no one else saw, but Jesus saw it and felt it. Peter's burden was the guilt and shame of having denied not lavish love for the Lord but mere association with him. Three times in that cold courtyard, Peter could not muster enough courage to claim his connection with the one he called Christ, Savior. Peter's threefold denial was redeemed by his threefold affirmation of Jesus.

Alan Jones, an Episcopal priest and writer, offers a wonderful perspective: God delights in us so much that the Holy Spirit is always "making us pregnant" with the new and unexpected by "unfitting us for things as they are." God's grace and mercy can bring us through. God can unfit us of things as they are in order to dress us for things as God would have them be.

Considerations and Resources

• Write the question "Do you love me?" twenty-five times. Each time you write the phrase, listen for something different. Incorporate what you hear in the message.

• Put yourself in Peter's shoes. What would starting over feel like for you? What do you really need to hear Jesus say?

• Consider preaching this message as a dialogue sermon.

My Thoughts and Ideas

Week Four

Our Hidden Power

Kirk Byron Jones

Text

Psalm 46:10*a*

Theme

To promote silence as a supreme underused spiritual discipline and practice.

Sermon Outline

OUR SUSPICION

• Stilled conversation, silence, is often seen as a sign of trouble.

• In spousal relationship, the weapon of choice is "the silent treatment."

• In the African American worship tradition, we have a way of attaching negative meanings to stillness and silence. If there is a lot of "Amen"-ing and singing and clapping, service must be good. If there is a more toned-down, hushed atmosphere, something is wrong.

STILLNESS IS NOT A NEGATIVE

Stillness is a positive thing; it is a necessary thing. It is not something to be suspicious of, but rather something to celebrate.

• Stillness is as an entranceway to deepening spirituality, to closer friendship with God.

- Jesus regularly practiced stillness: silence and solitude and time alone with himself and God.

PRACTICING STILLNESS EVERY DAY INVOLVES EMPTYING OURSELVES EVERY DAY

My native Louisiana is filled with swamps called bayous. Some of these swamps are rich in soil, foliage, and wildlife. Others are not so rich. The soil is contaminated and the life has been snuffed out by rot and stagnation. So there are good swamps and bad swamps. If we are not careful we can become people of the swamp of the latter variety. I have in mind our allowing ourselves to be filled longer than we need to be with the mental sludge of messy memories, grimy grudges, dirty doubts, and filthy fears—swamp stuff.

You know that you have experienced ultimate emptiness in your personal devotion when for a moment you are empty of words.

The Greater the Emptying, the Greater the Filling

> But those who wait for [wait on; wait with] the
> LORD shall renew their strength,
> they shall mount up with wings like eagles,
> they shall run and not be weary,
> they shall walk and not faint.
> (Isaiah 40:31)

Considerations and Resources

- Read and reflect on the following stillness moments of Jesus:
  - Matthew 13:1, "Jesus went out . . . and sat beside the sea."
  - Mark 1:35, "In the morning, . . . he got up and went out to a deserted place."
  - Luke 6:12, "He spent the night in prayer."
  - John 12:36, "He departed and hid from them."

• The legendary baseball pitcher Satchel Paige is also well known for his simple provocative sayings. Paige once said: "Sometimes you need to sit and think. And sometimes, you just need to sit." Reflect on this.

• In her wonderful book *When God Is Silent* (Cambridge, Mass.: Cowley Publications, 1998), Barbara Brown Taylor says that we have made Christianity "an overly talkative faith." Do you agree?

My Thoughts and Ideas

_____

_____

_____

_____

_____

Five Words for the Road

Text

Matthew 4:19, 28:10

Theme

To be re-encouraged by the earliest, simplest words of Jesus.

Sermon Outline

THE POWER OF SMALL WORDS

Games and lives can turn dramatically at the sound of a word or a phrase.

- Baseball: "Out" and "Safe."
- Weddings: "I do" and "I will."

Two thousand years ago, a man uttered two phrases (five words) that changed lives and ultimately changed history. He said them, and in a way he has never stopped saying them, and history has never stopped hearing them. While one phrase seeks to compel us, the other seeks to comfort us. While one phrase challenges us, the other encourages us.

"FOLLOW ME"

I was in a meeting the other day, and one woman playfully admonished another person she was supposed to be following to the meeting. "You left me," she said. "It was a good thing I had my navigation system on." Navigation systems are only recent installments in automobiles. In the past, if you got left, you got lost.

With Jesus, we don't have to worry about getting left behind. When it comes to following Jesus, the question is not are you fast enough, but are you faithful enough?

"Don't Be Afraid"

How can we not be afraid given our time of widespread violence and natural disasters?

There are no qualifying words in the Bible, no parenthetical disclaimers. "Do not be afraid" is not followed by "depending on the size of your challenges and difficulties." As we seek to resist fear, don't just remember the words "Don't be afraid," but remember the one speaking the words. The one doing the talking is the victor over sin and death.

A little boy couldn't sleep one night and called out to his mother. She answered. This call and response repeated itself several more times without the child saying anything. Finally the mother went in the child's room. When she asked him why he would not answer her, his response was, "I just wanted to hear your voice." Sometimes it's not so much the words, but the voice speaking that makes all the difference in the world.

Considerations and Resources

• The late Dr. E. V. Hill, longtime pastor of Mount Zion Missionary Baptist Church in Los Angeles, preached his wife's eulogy. During the eulogy, he told the story of praying that the Lord would spare his loved one's life. In his heart, he felt God encouraging him to faith and trust. After she passed away, he went back to God and asked for an explanation. Why had God asked him to trust while allowing his wife to die? Pastor Hill said that he heard the Spirit tell him: "E. V., when I told you to trust me, I meant I wanted you to trust me with her, out of your sight."

• Some consider fear to be the greatest obstacle to discovery and growth. Do you agree or disagree?

• Place yourself in the position of the first disciples. Would those five words have convinced you? Why? Why not?

- Use your imagination. If Jesus were alive in the flesh today, would he use the same five words to recruit followers? Can you imagine Jesus saying something different? Why? Why not?

My Thoughts and Ideas

_____

_____

_____

_____

_____

Week Five

Confronting Our Golden Calves

Kirk Byron Jones

Text

Exodus 32:1-10

Theme

To reflect on the nature of idolatry.

Sermon Outline

GOD AND MOSES

Something was wrong. According to Exodus 24:18, Moses had been on Mount Sinai forty days and nights. There was still no sign of him. He had been up there with God before, but never for that long. He usually went up into the mountain to speak with God (Exodus 19:3, 10; 24:9) and came down to give the people God's word (19:14). But this time, hours turned into days, days turned into weeks, more than a month, and no Moses. Something was wrong. Maybe God and Moses had hit a snag in their relationship. Perhaps they'd had a kind of falling out. Both of them were fairly intense and high-strung at times; both had tempers. Moses was a known killer (2:11-12). God had acted up so bad one day that the people were scared to death (20:18-19).

• Forty days and forty nights and not a sound from either one of them. Waiting turned to wondering, and wondering turned to worrying and fear.

- Why is it that the unknown can produce such fear inside of us?

NOT A REPLACEMENT; JUST A SUPPORT

The theme was not to replace the mighty and mysterious God of the mountain. This is clearly evident in their request to Aaron. They say to Aaron, the brother of Moses, the missing one, "Come, make gods for us, who shall go before us" Exodus 32:1).

In Exodus, "go before" is normally used in reference to God's messenger or God's special manifestation:

- 14:19: "The angel of God who was going before the Israelite army . . ."
- 23:23: "My angel goes in front of you."
- 32:34: "My angel shall go in front of you."
- 33:2: "I will send an angel before you."
- "Go before" is used in reference to the Lord who "went in front of them in a pillar of cloud by day, to lead them along the way, and in a pillar of fire by night, to give them light," in 13:21.
- "Go before" is reserved for messenger god (small g), and manifestation god (small g).
- "Go before" never referred to God (big G), the Ineffable, Unsayable, Unknown, Dynamic Essence Who inhabited the Mountain and All of Creation (big G God). The people did not have in mind replacing the God of the mountain. They wanted a "small-g God."

OUR "SMALL G" GODS

- Affluence
- Busyness

IDOLATRY UNCOVERED: TRYING TO SERVE "GOD" AND "GOD"

Aaron offers to make the god from the gold of their earrings. In their minds and hearts and in the idol itself, God will still be

in it. New god; no guilt. Then, to smooth things over with
Yahweh directly, Aaron suggests that when the calf is finished
they should bring it out, put an altar before it, and hold a "festi-
val to the Lord (Yahweh)." In other words, we'll praise both
God/gods at the same time.

• Idolatry is ascribing ultimate value to things of limited worth.
• Idolatry diminishes our opportunity for a deepening relationship with *God*.

Considerations and Resources

• Fear leads to idolatry. In his book *Awareness: A De Mello
Spirituality Conference in His Own Words*, Anthony De Mello
writes: "The first reaction [to something unfamiliar] is one of fear.
It's not that we fear the unknown. You cannot fear something
that you do not know. Nobody is afraid of the unknown. What
you really fear is the loss of the known" ([New York: Doubleday,
1990], 29). Do you agree with De Mello?

• In what sense did the people fear "the loss of the known" in
the text?

• What are some other candidates for "small g" god status?

• How does idolatry siphon off energy for an authentic relationship with the true and living God?

My Thoughts and Ideas

• Some idols I have struggled with include the following:

_____

_____

_____

_____

_____

Prayer Power

Marsha Brown Woodward

Text
Nehemiah 1:3-11

Theme
To celebrate and experience prayer's capacity to facilitate great accomplishments.

Sermon Outline
PRAYER AND GREAT WORK
Nehemiah was called to a great work. He heard that the people were in trouble, and his response was to pray and intercede, seeking to hear from God. Carlo Carretto says, "Whenever there is a crisis in the church it is always here: a crisis in contemplation" (Carlo Carretto, *The God Who Comes* [Maryknoll, N.Y.: Orbis Books, 1974]).

GOD: OUR FIRST OPTION
Nehemiah turns to God first as he sees the need to help and therefore seeks God as the first option instead of waiting until other options have been tried, which sometimes we can be tempted to do. Through both his times of prayer and fasting, he recognizes and affirms God's sovereignty for himself and the people he desires to help. He sees them all as being dependent on God.

WE PRAYER
Nehemiah identifies with the people by using *we* language, both acknowledges and accepts the corporate sin, and does not

blame someone else for the current situation but listens for how the situation can be changed. Nehemiah recognizes the whole of God's promises and commandments. He accepts the responsibilities that have been identified in the covenant that God made with Israel and is not just asking for God to intervene but to change them as well as the situation in light of the promises of the covenant.

THE DYNAMISM OF PRAYER

Prayer is dynamic because when we get serious about prayer, we start believing that God will move and act today in ways that God acted in past times.

• Many congregations have been birthed through prayer. If one looks back at the history of most congregations in their beginning, there was a prayer group, two or three or more individuals who gathered to seek God's will; and from that small group has come a congregation.

• Many times in the early years because of the dependency on God, the history is full of the things that were done and for which God was given the credit. Often as the congregation matures, God is given less credit, and people are given more credit.

THE DYNAMISM IN OUR SPIRITUAL DNA

If prayer is the root and foundation of a congregation and is in fact the DNA, then it is a part of our heritage to pray and to reclaim the dependency on God once held by the founders. Prayer may be the missing link in your congregation, the elusive something that has not been named but is keeping you from the next move of God and seasons of growth.

Considerations and Resources

• Have drawn or painted hands available in a variety of sizes, and ask the people to write a prayer request on a hand and place it in a prayer box. The hands may also be placed on the wall as a symbol of the commitments people are making to pray for the congregation and the needs of the community.

• Consider a silent walk around the community surrounding your congregation. As you walk, pray for each house, the people living there, and the situations they might be facing. If someone asks, the response is, "We are praying for *our* neighborhood." What a powerful witness!

• A variation would be to walk the streets asking God to give a fresh vision for the congregation as to how God wants to use the congregation in this community. Yet another variation is to drive through the neighborhood having one person drive while others in the car pray. This might be a way to involve all age groups: children praying for the children, youth praying for youth, young adults praying for those who are their ages, seniors praying for other seniors, and so on.

My Thoughts and Ideas

_____

_____

_____

_____

_____

MAY

ARTICLE

Preaching and Poverty

Gilbert H. Caldwell

The revelations of poor people and poverty in affluent America wrought by Hurricane Katrina cannot be avoided or ignored or dismissed by the preacher. Even as we know that quantitatively the face of poverty in the U.S.A. is white, the visibility of the black poor in New Orleans and in other places that were in the wake of Katrina cannot help leaving a lasting impression upon the preacher who holds the Bible in one hand and the newspaper in the other.

The opportunity for preaching about poverty is available to us in revisiting the "Poor People's Campaign" initiated by Martin Luther King Jr., which took place in Washington after his assassination on April 4, 1968. The failure of the Campaign to make a difference was about more than the absence of King to lead it. The PPC pulled together black, brown, and red poor people to challenge the nation's economic apartheid. The negative responses to it from some of the "friends" of the movement indicated that at bottom they could stomach and support the integration of black, brown, and red people into the existing social and economic order, but a challenge to the deficits of capitalism was greeted with "not in my neighborhood." Cries of "creating class warfare" were heard from right to left, from left to right.

We who are African American preachers in the twenty-first century must ask ourselves who of us would dare to lead a "poor people's campaign," considering our flirtations with economic success and the resultant "conspicuous consumption." Some of us would rather raise gently some of Martin King's intimate excesses than acknowledge the frugality of his economic lifestyle. We, with our salaries, expense accounts, luxurious houses, luxury cars, and so on, have not found ways to preach good news to the poor while vehemently contesting and condemning the conditions that make for systemic poverty in the first place. Our silence is part of the problem. The sad truth is, in some ways, when it comes to the causes of poverty, we have met the enemy and the enemy is us.

The April assassination date of Martin Luther King Jr., as he sought to lead Memphis garbage workers to economic independence, provides context for the pulpiteer. Preaching during that awful and awesome anniversary date of his death cannot avoid mentioning the May 1968 Poor People's Campaign.

MAY

SERMON OUTLINES

Week One

An Encouraging Word to a Discouraged Church

Charles Henry

Text

1 Corinthians 15:51-58

Theme

To celebrate strength in the midst of struggle.

Sermon Outline

THE POWER OF AN OLD LETTER

There is something about old letters that makes them difficult to destroy. The early church felt the same way about Paul's letters. Paul's letters had a personality that is unique. Paul opened his mind and heart as he wrestled with the issues that his beloved churches confronted. Paul's letters were to the point. Some of the same problems and crises that Paul wrote about over twenty centuries ago continue to frustrate the church fellowship.

THE CHURCH STRUGGLES AGAINST DISCOURAGING ODDS

- Division
- Immorality
- Extremism in the church
- Confusion

THERE ARE ENCOURAGEMENT RESOURCES

- Gratitude
- Redemption through Christ
- Abounding and delighting in the work of transformation

Considerations and Resources

- What is the (or your) church struggling against today?
- What does it mean to struggle well or to struggle poorly?
- Is disillusionment a sign of a lack of faith?
- What are your favorite faith encouragement resources? As a post-sermon exercise, ask congregants to list their favorite faith encouragement resources; include the list in the next church newsletter or post them on a message board.

My Thoughts and Ideas

What's Love Got to Do with It?

Gilbert H. Caldwell

Text

John 3:16

Theme

To engage the worshiping congregation in consideration, reflection, and exploration of the meaning and reality of the word *love*, which is too often trivialized, eroticized, and secularized. To misuse and misapply a word that is a centerpiece of the Christian faith is to trivialize, eroticize, and secularize God and what God has done in Jesus Christ.

Sermon Outline

EXPLORE LOVE PASSAGES

The preacher, as always, has the opportunity to arrange (and rearrange) the material presented to the listening/participating congregation. Sometimes, not always, an immediate exploration of the love passages in scripture is appropriate: Deuteronomy 11:1, Psalm 91:4-16, Song of Songs 1:5-7 (Why do African American preachers, or any preachers, avoid, "I am black and beautiful. . . . / Do not gaze at me because I am dark, / because the sun has gazed on me"?), Matthew 22:36-40, and 1 Corinthians 13:1-13.

EXPLORE LOVE IN "SECULAR" MUSIC

In this sermon, the preacher may first want to "touch base" with the congregation, awakening within their memories the use of the word *love* in so-called secular music. Jazz aficionados know John Coltrane's "A Love Supreme." Some of us, for a multiplicity of reasons (some good, some not so good), remember the words if not the name of the song that contains this declaration; "If loving you is wrong, I don't want to be right." Music of all kinds explores the genre of love.

We who want to connect with our listeners must risk reaching into and using the lyrics (and rhythms) of the music we do not often, or ever, hear in church. We who seek to proclaim a living Word and tell the "old, old story" must never contribute to the unnatural division between the so-called secular and so-called sacred. We are inauthentic, less than honest, and the quality of our "saved-ness" is in question if we avoid or run away from honesty and reality. We know that secular can become sacred, and we can turn the sacred into something less. I learned that forty years ago when I invited Duke Ellington and his orchestra to present his Sacred Concert at Union Methodist Church in Boston where I was Senior Minister.

Tina Turner, in her sixties at the time I write this, has, with her magnificent rendition of "What's Love Got To With It?" provided me with an opportunity to connect with and dissect common assumptions about love. In her song, she makes the statement, "Love is just a secondhand emotion." She also sings, "Who needs a heart when a heart can be broken?" The preacher responds, "Love is a firsthand emotion!" And hearts do not have to remain broken. The God in us and around us and within us makes love firsthand, and God is in the business of healing broken hearts. "Do I have a witness?"

MEANINGS OF LOVE

It is difficult to avoid those Greek words for love in this sermon. *Eros, philias,* and *agape* capture the breadth and meaning of love. Tragically, we have not always connected *eros* with love. Despite the enfleshment of the word *philias* in the name of the city of Philadelphia (the city of brotherly love *and* sisterly affection), too often neither the city nor we live up to the name in our lives. *Agape* is deeply embedded in the meaning of John 3:16. We follow Jesus; we affirm Jesus as Liberating Savior because our

hearts have been warmed and transformed by the presence of
God within him. That love of God in Jesus Christ is what makes
us who we claim to be.

LOVE AND JUSTICE

But love is not complete love if it does not have some manifestation in the existence of and the quest for *justice*. If we as preachers do not remember the words of Luke 4 that talk about what we
do when we are anointed by the Spirit, we preach an individualistic and capitalistic gospel that is unfaithful to the history, heritage, and hope that is ours as the African Diaspora in America!

Love has everything to do with everything because it is of *God*.
Christian sisters and brothers, "Don't even think about it" as
being anything else!

Considerations and Resources

• Frank A. Thomas, *What's Love Got to Do With It? Love,
Power, Sex, and God* (Valley Forge, Pa.: Judson Press, 2001).

• Alice Walker, *By the Light of My Father's Smile* (New York:
Random House, 1998)

My Thoughts and Ideas

_____

_____

_____

_____

_____

Week Two

MOTHER'S DAY

It's Only Mother's Nature

Teresa Fry Brown

Text

Matthew 15:21-27; Mark 7:24-30

Theme

To provide a balanced picture of African American mothers.

Sermon Outline

Mother's Day in the Black Church tradition is one of those worship opportunities to reach people who may not ordinarily attend. It is also historically a day when one is tempted to deify black mothers for their perseverance and love. The reality is that there are all types of mothers, some deserving of honor and some who have denied their privileged role.

- Definition, characteristics, and duties of mothers.
- Types of mothers—positive and negative examples.

THE TEXTS

- Compare and contrast Matthew 15 with Mark 7. Look for significant differences and similarities.
- Why was Jesus seeking a sabbatical? (What does the text teach us about ministry?)

152

- What is the sociocultural significance of the woman's origin?
- What is the significance of the context? What was the role of women in the culture? Where is the father?
- How did she know about Jesus?
- Was Jesus being rude in verse 27? Was Jesus caught in human cultural responses to the "other"?
- How far would you go as a parent to save your child?
- How do you feel after your child has been found, healed, and returned or grows up?

IMAGES OF MOTHERHOOD

- What associated biblical texts speak to motherhood or instruction of children?
- What cultural or congregational examples are there of motherhood not as exemplars, but as a normal range of motherhood?
- What are God's maternal characteristics (including disappointment and chastisement)?

Considerations and Resources

- Review the role of a mother in various cultures. Don't merely read; initiate conversations with mothers of various cultures.
- Read C. L. Franklin, "Hannah, the Ideal Mother" in *Give Me This Mountain: Life History and Selected Sermons* (Urbana: University of Illinois Press, 1989); Patricia Bell-Scott, *Double Stitch: Black Women Write about Mothers and Daughters* (Boston: Beacon Press, 1991); Teresa Fry Brown, *God Don't Like Ugly: African American Women Handing on Spiritual Values* (Nashville: Abingdon Press, 2000).
- Interview a child and a youth regarding their concept of motherhood or mother.
- Recognize that there are people in the congregation who do not have sound relationships with their mothers or whose mothers are deceased.

- Ask women of varying ages and family structures how they describe their life as mother. Include women who have not given birth to children but have "mothered" anyway.

My Thoughts and Ideas

_____

_____

_____

_____

_____

A Portrait of a Phenomenal Woman

Portia Wills Lee

Text

2 Kings 4:8-26

Theme

To celebrate spiritual greatness as expressed by great women of faith.

Sermon Outline

DEFINING PHENOMENALISM

In a society in which materialism is a norm, *who we are* is often based on whose name we're wearing or what we drive, where we live, and who we know. We must be conscious of what true phenomenalism is. It is an awareness of the Triune God as Creator, God as Jesus, God as Holy Spirit that makes us phenomenal, extraordinary, outstanding, and remarkable. It is our relationship with the phenomenal God that makes us phenomenal people.

When we view the portrait of a phenomenal woman, we see a woman who is elegant in many ways and in all she does. When we examine her portrait, we begin to understand what makes her this phenomenal woman. There are many women who come to mind for me when I see the portrait of a phenomenal woman: my mother, grandmothers, aunt, sister, cousins, friends, and neighbors.

However, there is one neighbor in particular, a woman who, with her dark, satin skin, silver hair halo, softness of height, proud walk, gentle talk, gifted hands, loving heart, and humble spirit, touches my heart the most because of her deep relationship with God. She reminds me of the woman in today's story. These women have attributes of focused priorities, family perseverance, and faith persuasion.

FOCUSED PRIORITIES MAKE US PHENOMENAL

• Spiritual perception. The Shunammite woman's relationship with God makes her perceptive to the needs of others.
• Service to others. She wanted to make sure Elisha had food and a place to stay.
• Satisfied with her position. She was content as a wife and a servant for God.

FAITH'S PERSUASION MAKES US PHENOMENAL

• Faith caused her to extend herself to others.
• Faith allowed her to believe Elisha when he said she would bear a son.
• Faith caused her to trust during adversity.

My neighbor, at ninety-five years old, still plays the organ for her church, cooks meals for the sick, visits the infirm in the hospital, and is still a portrait of a phenomenal woman. This phenomenal woman is still vibrant, while in the seasoned years of her life.

We, too, can join the ranks of countless other women when we do not allow our limitations to handicap us from being all that God has called us to be.

Considerations and Resources

• Consider the phenomenal women in your life; ponder their greatness and seek to include some of their testimonies in this message.
• Read poetry by Maya Angelou.
• Study the lives and words of great African American women such as: Zora Neale Hurston (writer), Mary Lou Williams (jazz composer and pianist), and Fannie Lou Hamer (civil rights leader).

My Thoughts and Ideas

_____

_____

_____

_____

Week Three

Touched by God for Greatness

Cheryl Kirk-Duggan

Text

Isaiah 6:1-8

Theme

As we are touched by God, we are called by God to touch others, to pass on that calling to every person and every church to embody and pass on God's touch.

Sermon Outline

ISAIAH'S BACKGROUND

The book of Isaiah attacks arrogance and hypocrisy, appeals to justice, proclaims God's sovereignty over history, and promises salvation to Israel and Judah.

Isaiah is an active, eloquent prophet from 742 to 701 B.C.E. in Jerusalem, the capital of Judah, southern kingdom, during the lives of four kings of Judah: Uzziah, Jotham, Ahaz, and Hezekiah.

Isaiah is a prophet closely related to Jerusalem's and Judah's aristocracy. Like a latter-day Colin Powell, Isaiah is the secretary of state to King Ahaz. Isaiah later seems to withdraw from public life. In times of crisis, Isaiah felt a weak Judah should go incognito and not participate in foreign alliances, as this was politically unproductive and religiously inappropriate. Israel should rely on God alone.

A Call Is a Commission That Names the Context for Our Relationship with God and One Another

- We are called to personhood.
- Each church has a unique calling.
- African Americans are called to witness of God's power and grace.

The Holiness of God Defines the Holiness We Are Called to Enact, Which Allows Us to Transcend the "Woe Factor"

- The holiness of God is the context and the process.
- Our inherited holiness is our motivation and covenant.
- Accepting holiness helps us transcend the mundane toward greatness.

The Touch of God Removes Our Iniquities, Our Sins, and Orchestrates Our Healings

- The touch of God convicts us toward mission.
- God's touch cleanses us and intensifies our capacity to see clearly.
- God's touch heals us and moves us toward transformation.

Considerations and Resources

- Isaiah's contact with the sacred is personal and powerful. What about his experience inspires you the most?
- "He Touched Me" is one of the familiar songs of the Black Church. Research the lyrics and the history of the song. Note other familiar religious songs with the element of divine touch.
- How do we invite God's touch? How and why might we run from God's hand?

- Note specific experiences when you have felt God's touch in your life; invite congregants to do the same.
- Reflect on the fear of and need for touching in our society.
- What is the power of a human touch? In what ways is a human touch similar to God's touch?
- How do we know when we have been touched by God?

My Thoughts and Ideas

_____

_____

_____

_____

_____

Flying, Walking, and Running: Three Forms of Divine Strength

Kirk Byron Jones

Text

Isaiah 40:27-31

Theme

To inspire strength for being, doing, and keeping the faith.

Sermon Outline

PUTTING IT INTO WORDS

- Have you ever had a taste for something, a deep yearning or desire that you could not articulate?

- Janet Fishburn, former Professor at Drew University, says, "The power of the prophetic figure is related to the ability of the prophet to verbalize a message which gives form to otherwise incoherent attitudes, reactions, and longings in the listener" (*The Fatherhood of God and the Victorian Family* [Philadelphia: Fortress Press, 1981], 12).

- Isaiah speaks to a nation ravaged by war and oppression as it stands at the dawning of a new day. The brilliance of the light of liberation is both energizing and blinding.

"THEY SHALL SOAR LIKE EAGLES"

This is the divine strength of ecstasy, abandon, celebration, and laughter.

- Everyday examples: bride and groom on their wedding day; an athlete in the "zone" or "flow"; a child on a playground.

- Biblical examples: David dances; the first Christians at Pentecost; the singing, soaring angels at the birth of Christ.
- We feel this strength in dynamic worship, wholehearted labor, and invigorating leisure.

"THEY SHALL RUN AND NOT BE WEARY"

This is the divine strength of day-to-day activism, the energy to accomplish, to do.

- This flies in the face of Karl Marx's classic critique of religion as having a numbing and dulling effect on people.
- At best, faith is a dance between Holy Spirit and human spirit. Sanctification is about not the obliteration of human initiative, but the enhancement of it. Purposefulness, initiative, and resolve are no less important to Christians than to anyone else.
- The church-based civil rights movement of the 1950s and 1960s is a shining example of the inspirational strength of activist faith.

"THEY SHALL WALK AND NOT FAINT"

This is the divine strength of endurance.

- The listing seems to be in reverse order. Should not the prophet have started with walking? Consider that the prophet's alignment is in order of importance in terms of frequency and difficulty. We walk more in life.
- The hardest thing to do is endure, especially when life seems to be coming apart at the seams.
- In *Black Womanist Ethics*, Katie Cannon celebrates the strengths of "indivisible dignity," "quiet grace," and "unshouted courage" (Atlanta: Scholars Press, 1988).
- Jesus in the Garden the night before his death.
- Lyrics to hymn, "I Want Jesus to Walk with Me."

Considerations and Resources

- Reflect on a variety of examples for the three forms of divine strength.
- Sometimes as preachers, we get stuck on the number three. What are some other possible forms of divine strength?
- What form has special meaning for you?
- How can you develop this theme into a sermon series?
- Strength is a term influenced by a variety of presumptions. Raise questions in your mind to deepen and enrich this sermon. Here are some to get you started: What is the nature of genuine strength? Is weakness the opposite of strength, or is it a different kind of strength? Who are the strongest people that you know or have ever known? What made them so strong?
- To get a firsthand account of the faith-based civil rights movement, read the classic *Stride Toward Freedom; The Montgomery Story* by Martin Luther King Jr. (New York: Harper, 1958).

My Thoughts and Ideas

_____

_____

_____

_____

_____

Week Four

Becoming Adventurous Ministers of God

Kirk Byron Jones

Text

1 Corinthians 12:4-6

Theme

To encourage risk in faithfulness.

Sermon Outline

MAN OF THE YEAR?

TIME magazine published four special issues over the past couple of years in which they've told the stories of individuals who have excelled in areas of life in this century. If *TIME* had been around during the building of the early church, the editors surely would have included Paul, the great evangelist/organizer of the infant church.

As Paul owned his giftedness, let us own our giftedness. In owning our gifts—accepting, practicing, and developing them—we do at least four things.

- We say "Thank you" to God.
- We bring pleasure to God. I rejoice in my children's soaring.

- We grow through a deepening commitment.
- We bless others.

SEEKING GREAT ADVENTURES

As Paul sought great adventures with God, let us seek to be great adventurers.

- Jesus' ministry hinged on those early disciples learning new skills.
- Don't just practice your gift skills; learn some new ones.

Considerations and Resources

- Study the word *adventure*.
- Develop a strategy for helping members of the congregation define and undertake new risks in their faith journey.

My Thoughts and Ideas

_____

_____

_____

_____

_____

Let Me Tell It!

Portia Wills Lee

Text
John 9:20-27

Theme
To encourage personal evangelism as a way of life.

Sermon Outline
THE DIVINE QUEST

God is constantly on a quest to provide a witness to God's self and greatness. People will find it a blessing to tell others about the lavish grace of God and God's goodness. It takes a profound trust to be able to witness for God, but more remarkable, God creates opportunities for us to gain the wisdom, trust, and hope to trust him, even against odds of retaliation and adversity.

PROBLEMS ARE USED BY GOD TO BRING GLORY TO GOD
- Even in the darkest situation, God may be glorified.
- Problems are disguised opportunities.

JESUS IS THE SIGHT GIVER
- Jesus heals.
- Healing cultivates faith.

THE CHALLENGES OF HEALING
- Suspicion
- Doubt

166

THE COMPULSION OF HEALING

- Claim your healing and testimony.
- Tell your story.

Considerations and Resources

- Research "testifying" in the African American religious experience.
- How do we share faith in inclusive as opposed to exclusive ways.
- Consider including a list of five to ten strategies for everyday witness.
- Institute a regular "Witness Workshop" at your church.

My Thoughts and Ideas

_____

_____

_____

_____

_____

JUNE

ARTICLES

The Enlivening Power of Reading

Kirk Byron Jones

I heard that legendary pastor/preacher/theologian Howard Thurman once told someone struggling over a career choice, "Do what makes you come alive. More than anything else, the world needs people who have come alive." One of the things that makes me come alive is reading. As a youth, I devoured books, especially biographies. Perhaps my initial fascination with books had to do with their power to transport me to places and times long ago. Through the years, my passion for reading has been fanned and fueled by a basic, incessant curiosity, a desire to have an adequate knowledge base from which to communicate with others and, most recently, a deepening appreciation for the craft of writing. (If you want to be mesmerized by a writer at his best, read *A Lesson Before Dying*, by Ernest J. Gaines, not just for its profound message but for its pointed eloquence [New York: A. A. Knopf, 1993]).

I feel blessed to be in a profession in which reading has long been considered an element essential to vocational faithfulness and effectiveness. Among the many benefits of reading for preaching are these: it nurtures thinking; it imparts varied and assorted kinds of knowledge; it develops vocabulary; it strengthens written and verbal communication; it sensitizes us to the meanings and sounds of words; and not least of all, it supplies material for more thorough, relevant, and convincing preaching.

As "wordsmiths of the Word," we cannot afford to ignore the importance of reading for overall spiritual development and intellectual stimulation, as well as for providing thoughts, phrases, and stories that may help us on any given Sunday bring the gospel home to heads and hearts. For me, one of the best moments in the study is reading something and knowing for sure that "this will preach." For example, last year I found a gem about hope that demanded inclusion in a sermon. In her short story

"Soon," Pam Durban writes about the life of Martha Crawford. Martha dreams and plans, but life does not work out as she expects. Still she keeps on keeping on, resisting the haunting temptation to become frigid to life. Durban goes on to describe Martha at a family reunion with something wonderful welling up inside of her:

> But there it was again, percolating up through the layers of years, bubbling out at Martha's feet like a perverse spring. This sly and relentless force that moved through the world, this patient and brutal something that people called hope, which would not be stopped, ever, in its work of knitting and piecing and binding, recovering, reclaiming, making whole. (Pam Durban, "Soon," in *The Best American Short Stories*, 1997, ed. E. Annie Proulx [Boston: Houghton Mifflin, 1997], 263)

I thank God for the joy and benefits of reading for living and for preaching. May the summer months provide you with respite, recreation, and good reading.

Preaching Goes to the Movies: Life Lessons from *Ray*

Kirk Byron Jones

R*ay*, a movie that brings to the big screen the big life of Ray
Charles, has drawn rave reviews. The effect goes beyond
Jamie Foxx's stunning performance, and even Charles's life
itself. The movie presents life lessons that can be used to enhance
greatly one's own living.

There is the lesson of finding your own voice. Ray Charles
enjoyed limited success early on because he sounded like singers
Charles Brown and the legendary Nat King Cole. Charles might
well have earned a sizable income by continuing to imitate these
great performers. But he had the good fortune of being challenged by Della Beatrice Robinson, his beloved "B," to "sound
like Ray Charles." It was only then that Charles began to let out
a blues-drenched, church-rinsed voice that had been building in
him all along. He had to choose to let it out, as we all must risk
being the person we really are in order to make our greatest contribution to society.

Another lesson presented in *Ray* is the importance of being
not just true to yourself, but also being open to who you are
becoming. Charles alarmed his record producer when, at the
height of his soul success, he opted to do a country and western
album. Charles argued that it was because of the soulful stories at
the root of country and western music that he had to do the
album. And besides, that music had been a part of his past and
was calling out for expression in the person he had become.

In my book *The Jazz of Preaching: How to Preach with Great
Freedom and Joy*, I discuss at length a jazz artist named Duke
Ellington who had a similar yearning for musical expansion and
evolution. Once, when asked to identify his favorite among his
two thousand–plus compositions, Ellington is said to have
replied, "My next one" (Nashville: Abingdon Press, 2004). We

cannot grow in life by holding on to familiar ways. Progress, not to mention excitement, comes in stretching forth, in launching out into more challenging and risky territory.

On a more personal note, I appreciated *Ray* affirming for me that religion does not have a monopoly on spirituality. I began preaching at the age of twelve in a Baptist church in New Orleans, Louisiana, where Charles lived briefly. While I was growing up in the church and pulpit, there was a time when I believed that God's Spirit was concentrated in these "holy places." No doubt, this belief fueled the fire of resistance from outraged congregants when Ray Charles began mixing church melodies with blues longings. They felt their music was being contaminated. Well, no one owns truly spiritual music. Preachers and other "saints" need to remember author Madeline L'Engle's words: "There is nothing so secular that it cannot be sacred" (*Walking on Water: Reflections on Faith and Art* [New York: Farrar, Straus and Giroux, 1980], 50).

Finally, *Ray* offers a poignant lesson about facing our fears. The first person to do this in the movie is Charles' titan of a mother, Aretha. She is the one who, after losing her youngest, George, stares squarely into Ray's unseeing eyes and challenges him to live an adventurous life in spite of his blindness. Ray Charles does just that, but along the way he finds himself haunted by a feeling of guilt regarding George's death.

In one of the movie's most dramatic scenes, Ray Charles's blindness is lifted momentarily, and he sees his dead mother and brother offering him sweet grace and courage. In his heart, he sees the loving truth that sets him free from fear. Stare your trouble in the face until it softens and shows you something that will set you free to live your best life. Ray Charles did, and the world is better for it.

JUNE

SERMON OUTLINES

Week One

Doing the Nineveh Thing!

Cheryl Kirk-Duggan

Text

Jonah 3

Theme

To celebrate telling and living God's Grace.

Sermon Outline

CAPTURED

Captured by Grace, Obedience, and Determination

Jonah tries to run away from God, a storm comes up, the sea becomes turbulent, Jonah is thrown overboard, and God sends out a big fish for Jonah's safety—three days, three nights.

- Are you running?
- Where/what is your fish?

Captured by the Word

Jonah prays a psalm of thanksgiving, from distress to consciousness of God's presence, to the voice of thanksgiving for deliverance.

- What is your distress?
- Have you experienced God's presence?
- For what can you cry out in thanksgiving?

In the text, we have a dialogical rhetoric, a conversation between God and Jonah, with clear, precise directions, requests, and invitations. When Jonah does not listen, God continues to call.

GOD HAS A CALL ON ALL OF OUR LIVES

Regardless of our vocation, gifts, or talents, God's call is an invitation to be obedient. Listen, get up, and go tell what God has told you to say. For the second time, God tells Jonah to go to Nineveh and cry out the message. How have you perceived God "going the extra mile" with you?

God's call on our lives to do the Nineveh thing is to practice our faith. As a recipient, Jonah, like us, is to listen, believe God, and practice his faith. The directions are specific; the divine voice says: "Tell it to the king."

Considerations and Resources

- How would you define the "Nineveh thing"?
- How do you preach obeying God in non-oppressive ways?
- To what extent are we called to partner with God in spreading "glad tidings of great joy"?
- Remember the features of your "calling." How can your testimony strengthen this message?
- Consider ways you can drastically present this sermon. How can you involve your youth in this whale of a story?
- Consider assuming the role of Jonah and preaching this sermon in the first person.

My Thoughts and Ideas

_____

_____

_____

_____

_____

Week Two

How John Saw Jesus

Charles Henry

Text

Revelation 5:6

Theme

To highlight and celebrate the various "faces of Jesus."

Sermon Outline

JESUS IN THE EYES OF HIS CONTEMPORARIES

When the Lord Jesus was here on earth, people had different views of him.

- Some saw him as an impostor. They cried, "Away with this man. Crucify him; crucify him."
- Some saw him as the "carpenter's son," just an ordinary laboring man with a special trade.
- Some saw him as a blasphemer.
- Some saw him as demon possessed; they said that he had a devil.

JOHN'S VISIONS OF JESUS

- John saw him as the wounded lamb.
- John saw Jesus as the worshiped lamb.
- John saw Jesus as the wedded lamb.

How Do You See Jesus?

- Is Jesus a lamb *to* you?
- Is Jesus a lamb *in* you?

Considerations and Resources

- Research the nature of lambs. Note the importance of the lamb metaphor for Jesus. In what ways was Jesus lamb-like?
- How do you make the lamb image live in an urban setting? Is there an alternative image that may be just as effective?
- How do you preach "lamb-ness" in such a way that it is not mistaken for weakness?
- How has your perception of Jesus changed over the years? Is an ever-changing perception of Jesus a sign of maturing faith?

My Thoughts and Ideas

A Great Big Little Thing

Kirk Byron Jones

Text

Luke 8:43-46

Theme

To trumpet the power of noticing small things.

Sermon Outline

JESUS NOTICES

After a class, a student once *shared sad* to me: "The doctors think that I have a serious lung illness, and I wanted you to know." I kept her in sight and saw that soon two other students surrounded her. I went over and asked if she wanted us to pray with her. She said, "Yes," and we held hands. Then she prayed first, "Lord, touch my body."

In the text, there is a woman who wants the Lord to touch her body. But she doesn't wait for the Lord to touch her. She reaches out and touches the Lord. One of the greatest miracles in the Bible takes place.

Jesus didn't know exactly what had happened, but he knew something did happen. This is the great big little thing. The great big thing is the healing; the great big little thing is Jesus *noticing*. Jesus was a great "noticer."

- He noticed the woman at the well.
- He noticed the child with a small lunch.
- He noticed the man in the tree.
- He noticed Mary and John at the cross.

WE SHOULD NOTICE MORE

- Lord, help us notice more. Our lives would be enhanced immensely, instantly, if we noticed more. Help us notice more the blessing of life.
- Count your blessings. Even tough times have lessons to teach us.
- Help us notice our loved ones more. In the last stages of a terminal illness, Michael Landon was asked if he loved his family more. Landon responded that he loved his family as much as he had always loved them. But he noticed them more.
- Thank God for noticing each of us.
- How can we notice God more?

Considerations and Resources

- In the week leading up to this sermon, keep a *small things* journal. Include some of your reflections in the sermon.
- Consider including practical exercises for becoming a better noticer. Here are some:
  - Study pictures and puzzles that ask you to find things that are hidden.
  - Read between the lines.
  - Listen to silence.
  - Slow down.

My Thoughts and Ideas

_____

_____

_____

_____

_____

Week Four

Name-calling

Portia Wills Lee

Text

Acts 11:26

Theme

To suggest that faithfulness is a matter of living up to and into our identity.

Sermon Outline

NAME-CALLING

Name-calling has traditionally been a way of defining a person, thing, or object. To have been called a name indicates that the name given at birth or as a term of endearment was not sufficient. It could also mean that what you are presently called is now insufficient for proper identification. Some names are called nicknames and some names are called pick names. All, however, seem to fit the recipient based on character or *behavior*.

NAMING FOR CHILDHOOD FUN

- Nicknaming was a testing.
- Nicknaming made people feel angry or special.

Naming Them Christian
- The named church was under persecution.
- The named followers appeared Jesus-like.

Living Up to Our Name
- Our name calls us to holiness.
- Our name calls us to sacrificial service.
- Our name calls us to be children of the Kingdom.

Considerations and Resources
- Recall nicknames from your childhood.
- Study the naming ritual in various cultures.
- African American religion has always celebrated "having a new name up in glory." What is the relationship between identity and freedom?

My Thoughts and Ideas

_____

_____

_____

_____

_____

JULY

ARTICLE

Hitting, Shedding, and Preaching

Kirk Byron Jones

I read somewhere that, between rounds of his unprecedented Masters victory, Tiger Woods spent a great deal of time hitting practice balls and practicing his swing. In a 1997 magazine interview, Pulitzer Prize–winning musician Wynton Marsalis attributed a great deal of his success to *shedding* or *woodshedding*, jazz slang for "practicing." Just think about it, two people who are regarded among the best of the best in their respective fields, still *practicing* their gifts day in and day out. As preachers, I think we can learn from their example.

Perhaps the greatest struggle of all in the pastoral ministry is carving out time for (1) regular study and (2) special study in preparation for Sunday's sermon (or sermons). Resistance to such necessary *sermonic shedding* comes from both without and within. From without, there are so many demands on us as pastors from the church and, increasingly these days in light of heightened political awareness of the social role of the church, from the community. Moreover, if you have what I call "the curse of the competent," a special ability to produce quality work in a timely fashion, you can literally busy yourself in some sort of ministry-related task twenty-four hours a day, seven days a week.

As pressing as the demands on our time may be, perhaps we ourselves pose the sternest resistance to regular study. Some ministers neglect study out of a negative valuation of their own intellectual abilities. They delude themselves into believing that they are simply not the studying type. Still others shirk study because of the isolated, quiet, "inactive" nature of it. They are used to moving about, getting things done, and identifying results; study is too passive. Perhaps the greatest deterrent to study is a distorted spirituality that diminishes intellect even though biblical religion prioritizes loving God with heart and mind.

How do we begin to make adequate time for *homiletical hitting?* First, I think one needs to be personally convinced about the importance of preparation for preaching. Harry Emerson Fosdick offers advice to Robert McCracken, his immediate successor at Riverside Church:

> Welcome to this church. It is a seven-day-a-week affair with more things going on here than you can possibly keep track of. Don't try to. Most of all we want your message in the pulpit, born out of long hours of study, meditation, and prayer. . . . What most of all we want from you is that on Sunday morning you should come into this pulpit here like Moses with the word of God, emerging from his communion on the mountain, who wist not that his face shone (Robert Moats Miller, *Harry Emerson Fosdick: Preacher, Pastor, Prophet* [New York: Oxford University Press, 1985], 334).

Second, every preacher needs to carve out fifteen to twenty hours each week for prayer, pondering, reading, writing, thinking, and rethinking—the stuff of our practice. Look at your schedule, identify the time when you are least likely to be interrupted, note it in your schedule as you would a meeting or visitation, announce it in writing to your congregation, and stick to it.

Why should golfers and musicians be more dedicated to their crafts than we are to ours? As we affirm the importance of preparation in preaching and develop and follow daily schedules that activate the affirmation, I believe the benefits will be great. Our God and our people will get more of the best we have to offer. Our preaching will be less stressful and more exciting. (Is there anything more torturous than trying to whip up a sermon for Sunday on Saturday night or, worse yet, on Sunday morning?) And we will experience what Bruce Mawhinney calls "reservoir power": "Preachers ought to be more like great reservoirs than mere water pipes. They should operate out of the fullness of God's presence in their lives rather than operating on the margin" (Bruce Mawhinney, *Preaching with Freshness* [Eugene, Ore.: Harvest House Publishers, 1991], 133).

July

JULY

SERMON OUTLINES

Week One

Sacred Place

Gilbert H. Caldwell

Text

John 5:2-4

Theme

To appreciate the sacred influence of setting.

Sermon Outline

SETTINGS

We are told of the location: Jerusalem. Where: by the Sheep Gate. What: there is a pool. Its name: Bethzatha. Its description: it has five porticoes. Who is there: many invalids. What about them: they are blind, lame, and paralyzed.

Location, location, location! Locations have a history, a reputation, a certain kind of ambience. New Orleans is the "Big Easy." (Why?) New York is the "Big Apple." (Why?) Chicago is the "Windy City." (Why?) Lou Rawls sings about "the Hawk," or the wind. Washington D.C. is "Chocolate City." (Why?) Los Angeles is the "City of Angels." (Why?) Philadelphia is the "City of Brotherly Love (and sisterly affection)." (Why?)

The specific place within the location: "There is a pool, called in Hebrew Bethzatha, which has five porticoes." Is there meaning in the name Bethzatha? Five porticoes? This provides an opportunity to talk about design, architecture, and the history of design and architecture and what it says about form and function.

BECOME INVOLVED

It is important not only to see, but also to feel and smell and become involved in what might be viewed as simply a place and nothing more. But "if the walls could talk." What names do we give the places that we visit? What reputations do places have, and are those reputations correct or misused?

In North Carolina in the 1930s, the town of Goldsboro was the location of the facility that housed the African Americans who were mentally and emotionally ill. Occasionally, when my behavior was less-than-perfect, I was threatened by some adult who said, "I'll send you to Goldsboro." (In retrospect, this threat was awful, wasn't it?)

FOLLOW JESUS

We follow a Jesus who was/is attentive to places as well as to people. The person of faith must never be inattentive. Never assume that "this is just another place for the sick." Never be oblivious to the effect the setting, the architecture, or the people have on those who are there and upon those who visit.

Considerations and Resources

• Research noted black architects, including Paul Williams and Benjamin Banniker.

• Speak of visiting hospitals, nursing homes, and so on. In my ministry, when I visited people in hospitals, homes, and on their jobs, I took notice of their physical environs, knowing that they were there 24/7 and were affected—knowingly or unknowingly—by the physicality of their location.

• Read *Outside Lies Magic: Regaining History and Awareness in Everyday Places* by John Stilgoe (New York: Walker and Co., 1998).

My Thoughts and Ideas

_____

_____

_____

_____

_____

Week Two

Where Is God in Illness?

Gilbert H. Caldwell

Text

John 5:5

Theme

To ponder new theological implications of illness.

Sermon Outline

ILLNESS AS DEFINING REALITY

Illness too often becomes our major defining reality, and the fact of our illness blots out all else, that we are someone else. How does one take note of illness, whether personal or of someone else, without letting the illness consume and dominate all that he or she is? Yet we cannot avoid the fact that illness is a major ingredient of life and we must live with it.

DISCOVER WHOLENESS

At times we may allow our illness to be an entry point to health, a different kind of health. Support groups for those with specific illnesses can be helpful in deepening one's understanding of one's illness but also can be a launching pad to discover a "wholeness" that transcends illness. Some cancer survivor support groups are now more optimistic, thankful, and joyful than are those groups that are supposedly health.

STEP OUT OF THE ILLNESS

Race for the Cure, which raises funds for breast cancer research, has become a celebration of survivors, their families, and supporters. Jerry Lewis's MDA Labor Day Telethon that raises money for children with muscular dystrophy is an activity of excitement and contribution. We are shaped by a human reality: humans want to contribute to cure, no matter what. Have we, ill or not, "stepped out of the illness" to do something to cure it?

FOREVER OUR COMPANION

Thirty-eight years and counting! When is the remembering of years helpful, and when is it harmful? How do we allow the "years of illness" to become a source of hope rather than a source of depression? What does "illness longevity" say about God's giving us the ability, capacity, and resiliency to survive and thrive? Jesus is forever our companion.

Considerations and Resources

• Is there a way for the preacher and the church to observe illness anniversaries in ways that are celebratory and liberating? How long have we and our church members lived with cancer, heart disease, and other illnesses? Why allow groups outside the church to be the only groups that acknowledge the reality of illness and find ways to help people "keep on keeping on" despite the illness? Is there the possibility that in the African American church, illness is another one of those "elephants in the middle of the room" we don't talk about?

• Why is it that wedding anniversaries are causes for celebration and we do not mind speaking the years from the rooftops? Birthdays, unless they celebrate many years or a few years, are not age specific. And yet we do not find ways to celebrate anniversaries of survival. If individuals who have been addicted to alcohol or other drugs can acknowledge how many years they have been "free and liberated," why cannot folk with other illnesses?

• Have a conversation with someone who has lived with illness for many years. Catalogue your learning; seek to incorporate him or her into this message.

• What is your own experience with illness?

My Thoughts and Ideas

_____

_____

_____

_____

_____

Week Three

The Jesus Question

Gilbert H. Caldwell

Text

John 5:6

Theme

To explore the importance of genuine desire for healing and transformation.

Sermon Outline

BEDSIDE MANNER

What do we think of the bedside/poolside manners of Jesus? "Do you want to be healed?" What kind of question was that? Is this the first question you ask when you are visiting someone in the hospital for the first time or someone who has been in the hospital for a long time? You and I may not, but then, we are not Jesus!

JESUS KNEW

Jesus knew the man's illness history. How do we think he knew? Did one of the attendants at the pool pull out the man's chart and give it to Jesus? Did some "gossip" at the pool whisper to Jesus and say, "That fellow over there has been here for a long time, and sometimes he acts as though he owns the place?"

ALL KINDS OF GIFTS

Some of us believe that Jesus was gifted with all kinds of gifts: the gift of intuition, the gift of "sizing up people" quickly, and the gift of an immediate kind of empathy with people. (The illustrations are numerous: the woman at the well, Zaccheus, the disciples, and so on.)

WHAT DO YOU WANT?

The question above all questions is: "Do you want to be made well (healed)?" Everybody claims they want to be healed, but do they? The Spiritual says, "Everybody talking about heaven, ain't going there." We say with our lips often what we do not mean in our hearts.

"I want to lose weight." But we do not do what we ought to do to lose weight.

"I want to deepen my faith." But we avoid the disciplines that deepen faith: confession, prayer, Bible study, personal and corporate worship, service to others, involvement in challenging the principalities and powers that oppress. I am a witness that in Mississippi at Selma and on the streets of Chester and Boston, my faith was deepened. Risk-taking involvement—not because it is "politically correct," but because it is "theologically correct,"—has a way of deepening faith.

LIVING THE JESUS QUESTION

Years ago, Robert Raines wrote the book, *Living the Questions* (Waco, Tex.: Word Books, 1976). Each day of our lives we must live *the Jesus question*, "Do I want to be healed?" More than ever, we of the African Diaspora in America must ask about our communities, "Do we want healing and healed communities, or do we want to 'talk the talk and not walk the walk?'" How do you and I answer *the Jesus question?*

Considerations and Resources

- Read or survey *Living the Questions* by Robert Raines.
- Identify some other significant questions of Jesus in Scripture.
- Reflect on ways you can incorporate more questioning into your preaching.
- Read or survey *The 7 Powers of Questions: Secrets to Successful Communication in Life and at Work* by Dorothy Leads (New York: Berkley Group, 2000).

My Thoughts and Ideas

_____

_____

_____

_____

_____

Week Four

Healing Stories

Gilbert H. Caldwell

Text
John 5:7

Theme
To celebrate the power of our healing testimonies and stories.

Sermon Outline

NOTHING ELSE TO TALK ABOUT?

When does sharing/telling our illness history move from imparting historical information to becoming a continuous "pity party" that we want others to become a part of? The sick man sought to justify his thirty-eight years at the pool. He may have wanted to see in the eyes of Jesus the signs of sadness over his plight. We must always ask ourselves, "Am I answering questions that nobody is asking?" Or have we been telling the same story for so long that we have nothing else to talk about?

STIRRING UP THE WATER

"When the water is stirred up" offers individual sermon possibilities in itself. Stirred-up water in whirlpool baths, washing machines, and dishwashers is necessary for healing and cleaning. How much should worship be "stirred up" in order to be worship? On the one hand, sometimes the "stirring up" in worship is so obviously manipulated that the healing it promises and delivers is bogus.

On the other hand, what about worship that is not "stirred up," either because there is fear of "losing complete control" or because folk feel that "stirred-up" worship is incompatible with their intellect or their status? One of the challenges of black worship is sometimes the length of black worship! Some say the length of worship is necessary in order to allow the Spirit that stirs to come by.

THE PREACHER AS STORYTELLER

The preacher as a "storyteller" is challenged to assist others in telling their stories in ways that are informational as well as inspirational! The preacher as the spiritual *Griot* has an opportunity to assist folk in finding their stories, unearthing them, and then telling them in ways that give evidence of the faith that is in them.

MY SOUL IS RESTED

Suppose the "sick brother" had answered Jesus by saying, "I have been blessed" or "I'm too blessed to be stressed" or "My body is tired, but my soul is rested." Remember during the Montgomery bus boycott, the woman, Sister Pollard, who said, "My feet are tired, but my soul is rested." The stories we tell and the way we tell them heal our todays and tomorrows.

Considerations and Resources

- Identify the hallmarks of great storytelling.
- Interview a great storyteller in your family or congregation. Ask him or her to share with you "the tricks of the trade."
- Read *Improving Your Storytelling: Beyond the Basics for All Who Tell Stories in Work or Play* by Doug Lipman (Little Rock: August House, 1999).

• Why do you think storytelling was so important to the preaching of Jesus? How much do you rely on storytelling in your own preaching?

My Thoughts and Ideas

_____

_____

_____

_____

_____

Week Five

Stand Up!

Gilbert H. Caldwell

Text

John 5:8-9

Theme

To affirm divinely inspired human initiative.

Sermon Outline

A SHOUT "COMING ON"

Sometimes, a Scripture text is so powerful and liberating that it provokes and evokes a "hallelujah, amen" just by reading it and hearing it and reading it and hearing it again. It is good for the preacher to know that the Word is the source of joy, liberation, and power and not his or her pulpit eloquence or elegance. Quiet United Methodist that I am, even I feel a shout "coming on" as I read and write and feel this text. In my senior years, I am experiencing more of the presence of God and more worship at my computer than I ever did when I had a weekly sermon to produce and preach. Never, never disregard or avoid the worship that takes place during the moments of preparation and the preparation that produces worship, days before the Sunday morning "moment."

"Doctor Jesus" has let loose the liberating and healing medication that is resident in the gospel and supposedly lived by the Gospel messengers as they proclaim it Sunday after Sunday.

201

No Timidity

"Stand up!" There was not a question mark but an exclamation mark at the end of this order. Preachers are always challenged to be so sure of the message they have received that there is no timidity in the telling of it. "Stand up!" is a command that first must be received internally before it can be acted upon externally. So many folk, because of their faith, are able to stand up internally even though physically they cannot, or when they do stand up, their legs are unsteady.

The little boy played all morning with his birthday toy. It was a toy soldier that would bounce back up when he hit it. Late in the morning, he went to his father and asked, "Daddy, why does he bounce back up, no matter how hard I hit him?" The daddy did not know or was too busy to answer. The boy filled the empty space left by his father's silence by saying: "I know why he bounces back up, no matter how hard I hit him. He's standing up on the inside." Was it not the apostle Paul who said, "Though I have been knocked down, I have not been knocked out."

Take Up Your Mat

"Wellness" comes when we decide to "take up our mat." When we do so in response to the message delivered by God through Jesus, we are not only following a divine order, but also taking personal control of something that may have restricted and impeded us, despite the comfort it produced.

Command and Response

Responding to the liberating and saving word that is the gospel heals us in ways that transcend the physical. Spirit does what the body may be unable to do. This is a scripture of *command and response*. What a magnificent response!

Considerations and Resources

• Martin Luther King Jr. warned against depending on inevitability to bring about progress. What do you think about this sentiment?

• Reflect on the relationship between grace and human initiative in your life.

• How do you reconcile texts such as "Stand still, and see the salvation of the LORD" (Exodus 14:13 KJV) with "Stand up"?

My Thoughts and Ideas

_____

_____

_____

_____

_____

AUGUST

ARTICLE

The Paradox of Paradise: Preaching and Practicing the Kingdom

Jeffrey L. Brown

Luke 23:39-43

I have three children, ages eight, five, and three years. One day, I took them to nearby Raymond Park to swing. I like this park because it has three swings in a row. Each child has a swing. While I was pushing the three of them upward to the sky, my oldest daughter asked me a question: "Daddy, what is heaven on earth?" The statement momentarily stunned me. Upon recovering, I asked, "Why?" She told me that she heard a song by a group called *Solo.* Since the song included the words, "I got heaven right here on earth," she wanted to know "what was heaven on earth?" I assured her that heaven was not what the song suggested it was. Now, when you answer a child's question you must expect another, if not a barrage of questions. I got a barrage: "What's heaven like?" "What do people do in heaven?" "What happens when you get bored in heaven?" "Do they have candy there?" As if his sister's questions were not enough, my five-year-old joined in, "Can I bring my trucks to heaven?"

Let me ask you some questions. What is your concept of paradise? How do you envision heaven? Where do you see it? Those of you just entering seminary should expect to tackle these questions in a more sophisticated way. Those of you exiting seminary will have these questions posed to you in churches, mission fields, and hospitals, just to name a few places.

For many of us, going to the Bahamas would make us feel like we were in heaven, a place a total contentment, peace, joy, and happiness. And if we were honest, we would admit that realized personal bliss is the heaven that most of us try to achieve in life. To our credit, we do not just see heaven in terms of our personal peace, but in the spread of social peace and justice. We have sufficient biblical witness for this heaven. No less than the public ministry of Jesus begins with the proclamation that the "reign of

God" or the "kingdom of heaven" is not some inaccessible place in the sky, but is "at hand."

For many, "paradise" is the attainment of "the American dream." The dream has many versions. While former presidential aspirant Bob Dole declared that he would help deliver the dream to America by reducing taxes, increasing the military budget, balancing the federal budget, protecting social security, and building more jails. Ironically (given the last item on the agenda), he ended by referring to himself as "the most optimistic man in America."

Martin Luther King Jr. articulated another, more eloquent version of the dream for a better nation in 1963. King saw the development of a nonsegregated nation as an important step toward "the beloved community." King imagined that "little black boys and black girls will be able to join hands with little white boys and white girls as sisters and brothers" ("I Have A Dream," in *A Testament of Hope*, ed. James Washington [San Francisco: HarperSanFrancisco, 1991], 219).

So it is that in various, often opposing, ways, it has been the dream of America to seek after paradise, to find a little heaven right here on earth. Some would argue that this is as it should be. Paradise is having a "piece of the pie" in this land of opportunity. And why not? It harmonizes with our praise of rugged individualism and our uncritical devotion to market capitalism. Yet paradise envisioned primarily if not solely as economic prosperity in the United States is challenged by the reality of widespread economic and social disparity in our country. We see the nihilism in the eyes of young people in our streets and the poverty and growing despair that cuts across race, class, and gender.

We have, while others do not. We hope, while others will not. Though we can try to hide behind the language of self-help and self-responsibility and the rhetoric of welfare reform and budget balancing, the questions still linger in the back of our minds: Is this the best approach for humanity? Will we achieve the beloved community in this way? Is this the moral path that God intends for us to follow? Are we truly following the path to paradise?

Martin Luther King Jr., who followed the teachings of Jesus and the ideology of Ghandi, would tell you that paradise is not found in the American dream or the Protestant work ethic or market capitalism. He would tell you that it is not even found in the Bahamas! In fact, King would warn against identifying paradise with any system or tangible thing. Moreover, I think he would tell us that in order to enter paradise we must not obsessively seek after it, but live its paradox.

This is what intrigues me about one of the thieves condemned to die in Luke 23:39-43. I do not know whether or not there was a "three strikes and you're out" criminal justice policy two thousand years ago; but one thing is certain: the thief is facing the ultimate penalty, which is death, specifically death on the cross, "an event" of pain on display that people watched as casually as we view violence on television today. The thief realized that whatever else had happened in his life, he had not realized his personal paradise on earth, and the clear signal of his failure was his public beheading, his death on the cross. The humility and glory of this thief is that he owned his failure. "We deserve this," he admitted. Then he looked at Jesus and explored the paradox of paradise, saying, "But this man has done nothing wrong." The thief then entered into the paradox with the words, "Remember me when you enter into your kingdom." What is the paradox of paradise? It lies in the willingness to lose the paradise you create (or try to create) in order to gain the true paradise. To live the paradox of paradise is to give up your right to paradise in order to reap it.

To live the paradox of paradise in terms of social justice is to give up our personal *comfortability* (our created paradises) in order to work toward a greater paradise of justice for all of God's children. The pursuit of this paradise is not devoid of all self-interest. How many of us are willing to risk our paradise, whatever it might be, to help save our children?

Dr. James Alan Fox, dean of the college of criminal justice at Northeastern University, has written an eye-opening document entitled "Reporting on Trends in Juvenile Violence"

(Bureau of Justice Statistics, Oct. 1–Dec. 31, 1995). He says that even though the overall murder rate has declined 4 percent between 1990 and 1994, the murder rate among teens aged fourteen to seventeen has increased 22 percent. There are currently 39 million children in this country under the age of ten (the most in fifty years). It is being predicted that by the year 2005 the number will increase by 20 percent. Fox concludes that this growth in the youth population mixed with growing youth violence places us on the brink of an unprecedented juvenile crime wave.

Instead of children who grow up with the strength of character, discipline, a thirst for literacy, and faith and hope for the future, many of our children are growing up in the ruins of distorted values, a violent drug culture, and an economy driven by self-interest. The result is soaring numbers of young adults with deferred dreams and fractured futures. Although most prominent in the inner cities, this mark of the beast of violence has found its reach into every ethnic community, in the outermost corners of the nation, and in the rural hamlets and suburban enclaves of the United States.

Whether you believe that this is a result of pervasive systemic oppression or the failure of Great Society government, one thing is for sure: there is a genuine crisis in our land concerning youth violence, and it is getting worse.

Beyond the political polarizing discussions about the rebuilding of society, faith-based communities must take an active role at the table if society is to make any real headway in the advancement of public policy into the twenty-first century. We must give up all notions of paradise that prevent us from actively healing our children, meeting them where they are and not waiting for them to come to us. This is the compelling motive behind the Ten-Point Coalition, a Boston-based coalition of religious leaders, which has called churches to concentrate their energies in one or more of the following priorities:

1. Adopting youth gangs.

2. Sending mediators and mentors for black and Latino juveniles into the local courts, schools, juvenile detention facilities, and streets.
3. Commissioning youth workers to do street-level work with drug dealers.
4. Developing concrete economic alternatives to the drug economy.
5. Building linkages between downtown and suburban churches and inner-city churches and ministries.
6. Initiating and supporting neighborhood crime watches.
7. Developing partnerships between churches and community health centers.
8. Establishing brotherhoods and sisterhoods as a rational alternative to violent gang life.
9. Establishing rape crisis drop-in centers, services for battered women, and counseling for abusive men.
10. Developing a black and Latino history curriculum, with an additional focus on the struggles of women and poor people as a means of increasing literacy and enhancing self-esteem in young people.

What is needed is sacrifice, the sacrifice of paradise (our comfortable confines and race, class, and gender prejudices) for the paradise of the liberation and healing of our children. We must move quickly to live the paradox of paradise, to tackle head-on the problem of youth violence and hopelessness, believing that it is possible to turn around those youth we have written off. The question is not will the violence and despair go away, but rather how much of ourselves are we willing to commit so that we will not have to refer to our time as the transition between postmodernism and catastrophe?

In his book *Denial of Death*, Ernst Becker writes that the urge within to cosmic heroism is sacred and mysterious and cannot be neatly ordered and rationalized by science and secularism (New York: Free Press, 1973). The only steps that can change society are heroic ones. How many are willing to risk their paradise in order to gain it?

AUGUST

SERMON OUTLINES

Week One

Use It or Lose It

Charles Henry

Text

Matthew 25:14-30

Theme

To encourage full use of our gifts to God's glory.

Sermon Outline

THE NATURE AND NUMBER OF THE TALENTS

- Ownership was undisputed.
- Value was incalculable.
- Trust was inestimable.

THE USE AND ABUSE OF THE TALENTS

- If properly used, the talents had the potential to be increased.
- If improperly used, the talents would be diminished.

THE RETURN AND REWARD OF THE MASTER

- The return of the master is assured.
- There was a great reward for the servants who used their talents wisely.
- There was great disappointment for the servant who had not used the talents with which he was entrusted.

Considerations and Resources

- Do a study of "talents" in Scripture.
- Do an inventory of gifts you claim and have used through-out your life. Assist your congregation in doing the same.
- How do gifts expand us as individuals and congregations?
- As marvelous as gifts are, there is a shadow side associated with their use. Some people operate out of their gifts so much that they barely have time to rest and simply be who they are apart from their gifts. How can you integrate this gift-corrective into the body of this message?

My Thoughts and Ideas

_____

_____

_____

_____

_____

Week Two

Omission or Commission?

Teresa Fry Brown

Text

Matthew 25:31-46

Theme

To remember or reconnect with baptismal and ordination vows.

Sermon Outline

UNDERSTANDING MISSION

The ordination process in many denominations involves questions of call, belief, anointing, appointments, authority, gifts, talents, leadership, submission to superiors, and ministerial education. The biblical text designates the overarching attribute of ministry as love of the believers, God's children, or the membership. The focus text outlines this important aspect of our mission. What is the mission of contemporary ministries, churches, denominations, religious organizations, or multimedia programs?

CONTEXTUALIZATION

• What lessons or teachings immediately preceded this parable?
• Who is included in the call to ministry?
• Who or what illustrates sheep and goats? What is the different between the behavior of a sheep and that of a goat?

- How important is judgment to understanding the parable? Whose judgment?

JESUS DEFINES MINISTRY

- Verse 45 is crucial to the commission.
- Are there other texts that echo the sentiments in this passage?
- What types of love are necessary for ministers?

ABDICATION VS. ACQUIESCENCE

- What happens when we accept our mission?
- What happens when we reject our assignment?
- What are we willing to risk to live into our ministries?
- What is the reinforcement for continuing in ministry?

REMEMBERING

End with recitation of baptismal or ordination vows as a reminder of acceptance of the mission.

Considerations and Resources

- Read *We Have This Ministry: The Heart of the Pastor's Vocation* by Samuel Proctor and Gardner Taylor (Valley Forge, Pa.: Judson Press, 1996). Keep a journal of your ministerial experience. Interview/talk with other ministers about their experiences to authenticate claims on the text.
- Research denominational ordination litanies and baptismal rituals. Develop reaffirmation services particular to one's denomination using this text or similar texts.
- Read *How to Preach a Parable: Designs for Narrative Sermons* (Nashville: Abingdon Press, 1989) by Eugene Lowry and *Parables for Preachers* by Barbara Reid (Collegeville, Minn.: Liturgical Press, 1999).

My Thoughts and Ideas

Week Three

The Three Blessings in Every Storm

Kirk Byron Jones

Text

Mark 4:35-39

Theme

To encourage hopeful strength in adversity.

Sermon Outline

STORMS

As a child, the onset of stormy weather set off a spirit of play inside of my brothers and me. The sprinkling rain, darkening skies, and strong winds would set off something inside of us, and we would run out to the vacant grass lot next door and start playing "running through." We would throw a football in the air, and whoever caught it started running around the lot until he was tackled. We'd romp and run until our mother's voice rang out: "You better get in this house."

Storms really aren't playthings. There were severe storms as I was growing up in New Orleans.

THREE BLESSINGS IN EVERY STORM

• God's Abiding Presence: Through it all, Jesus never leaves the boat. Jesus will never leave us alone.

- God's Keeping Presence: Jesus kept the disciples throughout the storm's duration. No matter how long our storms, God will keep us.
- God's Delivering Presence: Jesus calmed the storm. God is still calming storms.

Considerations and Resources

- Review some of the great "storm songs" of the faith. Here is one:

> When the storms of life are raging, (stand by me)
> when the storms of life are raging (stand by me)
> When the world is like a ship upon the sea,
> thou who rulest winds and waters (stand by me).
> (Charles Albert Tindley, ca. 1906)

- Reflect on the challenge of preaching about adversity without minimizing its hurt and pain.
- Read James Cone's *The Spirituals and the Blues: An Interpretation* (Westport, Conn.: Greenwood Press, 1980).

My Thoughts and Ideas

_____

_____

_____

_____

_____

Week Four

How to Have Peace in the Storm

Kirk Byron Jones

Text

Mark 4:35-41

Theme

To claim the peace that is ours in every situation, no matter how stormy.

Sermon Outline

THE STORM

- Storms happened suddenly on the Sea of Galilee, due to its low level, the warm climate, the surrounding hills and valleys, and the sudden arrival of cold air. Sudden storms happen in our lives.

- Not just suddenness, but the violent nature of the storm is an issue. The text suggests it was a "tempest," earthquake-like. There are storms and there are *storms*. Some things turn our lives upside down and inside out.

- At the farthest reach of their fear, they remember something: Jesus is on board.

PEACE IN THE STORM

Jesus was in the back of the boat. We need to spend more time in the back of the boat, celebrating sacred leisure.

• We live amid storms of overcommitment and hurry. Dr. Richard Swenson refers to this as "living without enough margin, space between ourselves in our limits." Recommend *Margin: Restoring Emotional, Physical, Financial, and Time Reserves to Overloaded Lives* (rev. ed., Colorado Springs, Colo.: NavPress, 2004).

• Practice Sabbath. Doing so would place us in a better state when storms arrive.

• Jesus was sleeping in the back of the boat; we can rest in the storm.

• Practice "sanctified negligence." Sometimes the best thing to do in a crisis is nothing at all.

• We can rest in the eye of the storm, "God's Eye": complete trust in God.

• Read the lyrics to Thomas Dorsey's classic storm-resting song, "Precious Lord, Take My Hand." Jesus talked to (rebuked) his storm. Learn how to talk with an attitude to your storm.

• Talk to your storms in a way that proclaims victory, power, and authority over them.

• Isaiah 26:3: "Thou wilt keep him in perfect peace, whose mind is stayed on thee" (KJV). We can choose our mental state. We can choose peace.

• Claim the peace that is yours in every situation, no matter how stormy.

Considerations and Resources

• Reflect on some of your biggest storms; be honest about your struggle and pain. Journal about current storms you may be going through.

• Research songs/scriptures that refer to storms. One of the most well known is Charles Tinley's "Stand by Me."

• Consult *Rest in the Storm: Self-care Strategies for Clergy and Other Caregivers* by Kirk Byron Jones (Valley Forge, Pa.: Judson Press, 2001).

• Howard Thurman once concluded after a personal storm, "I need never fear the darkness, nor delude myself that the contra-

dictions of life are final" (*With Head and Heart: The Autobiography of Howard Thurman* [New York: Harcourt Brace Jovanovich, 1979], 83). What do you hear in this declaration?
  • Recall storms of the recent past that have devastated towns and cities, including New Orleans. Think about how you can preach persuasively, yet sensitively and compassionately, about storms.

My Thoughts and Ideas

_____

_____

_____

_____

_____

September

SEPTEMBER

Claiming Creativity for Preaching

Excerpted from The Jazz of Preaching:
How to Preach with Great Freedom and Joy
(Nashville: Abingdon Press, 2004) by Kirk Byron Jones

Why is the passion of creativity so regularly associated with jazz so foreign from discourse about preaching? What dries up creative juices in preaching? Why might we be resistant to granting creativity a more substantial role in the preaching process?

Two unsuspecting beliefs may be mostly responsible for creativity's muting in preaching: *the belief that preaching is mainly receiving God's word* and *the belief that we preach a gospel that essentially remains the same.*

For some, to allow too much human involvement in preaching, including creative ingenuity, is to poison the preaching possibility. Preaching is God speaking through humans. While we hear and appreciate the necessary deference to divinity, such deference can lapse into negligence. If preaching is God's baby, then let God feed and diaper the baby. One's own responsibility for nurturing compelling, provocative sermons can be undercut by rigidly fixating on God as preaching's ultimate source and inspiration.

You'll get no argument from me about God's ultimate responsibility for preaching. But what if the call to preach includes permission to interpret the word in manifold, meaningful, and magnificent ways? What if God is ever watchful, like a child looking up the street for a parade, to see how the word will be adorned and borne, afresh and anew? It's not just that we have a waiting congregation every time we preach, but a waiting God. What if God smiles when we preach not just because we have been true to the script, but because, through God's gift of creativity, we have been true to the script in fresh new ways?

Creative preaching may be unconsciously squelched by adherence to an ironclad, closed understanding of the Gospel. I remember hearing preachers of my childhood preach about Jesus who was, in biblical parlance, "the same yesterday, today, and tomorrow." Unfortunately, the same description could be applied to some of their preaching. Inadvertently, the same old story led to the same old telling.

Even if one grants a sense of sameness and even finality to God's redemptive work in Christ Jesus, it is always possible to widen our vision of God's labor of grace. We can regularly preach new dimensions of the "unchanged" faith experience, and preach it in novel ways. Even if you must believe that the word has not changed, you must grant that our apprehension of the word is constantly changing, and the Word behind the word has never been fully comprehended. What if after 2000 years of preaching, we have yet to scratch the surface in terms of comprehending and construing ways of telling the story? What if God is waiting with tiptoe-expectancy for us to creatively see and seize these new ways?

Unleashing the Creative Impulse

Creativity in preaching begins with lavish portions of personhood and permission.

Human beings are an extraordinarily creative species. The trouble is that most of us never approach the vast expanse of our creative capacities. Scientists tell us that we use only 10% of our mental capacity. Most of us sleep with our creative limitation. We are discouraged daily by crushing societal reminders of what we cannot do. The first step in becoming a more creative preacher is embracing your status as a creative individual. The proof of your creative genius is not in your ability to paint stunning pictures or write stirring musical compositions, but in your ability to imagine, and playfully construct. To the extent that all of us can imagine and make, we all are creative—most of us to a measure beyond our widest dreams.

Creativity flourishes when we dare to be, freely and fully, our genuinely creative selves. Creative preaching, free and insightful sermonizing, comes more easily and regularly from free people. A free person is someone who has accepted their acceptance from God and life. Having received this fundamental acceptance, they are free to route their energies into creative expression as opposed to constructing personal and interpersonal defenses and denials: the fatiguing work we do when we are not at home with who we are.

Owning your capacity to create must be followed by granting yourself permission to do so. Here is where the jazz musician is such a wonderful model for the preacher. Who authorized Louis Armstrong to play with such passion, precision, and power? And who gave him the permission to put gravel in his voice, and sing in a way that no one had sung before? What gave Sarah Vaughn the right to assume that her voice was no less an instrument than Armstrong's trumpet? How dare she have the audacity to think that she could master control over her voice in the same way that a musician honorably tames and rides her instrument? Where did such creative authorization derive? The authority came from Within and Without, the former being no less sacred than the latter. Receiving permission for creative preaching means believing that the Spirit is delighted with our daring to hear and tell the Gospel in fresh new ways, in ways that cause God to smile.

Once, as I was observing morning devotion, I began stretching my arm forward to get some of the waking-up kinks out. I did this several times. The last time I stretched forth my arm, I realized that I was moving it toward the place where a small candle sat burning. When it comes to creativity, the great challenge is to reach for the flame, to embrace the fire (pp. 67-70).

September

SERMON OUTLINES

Week One

Finding Joy in Our Work

Kirk Byron Jones

Text

Luke 10:1-2, 17

Theme

To link work-joy with continuous learning.

Sermon Outline

BEFORE-MISSION AND AFTER-MISSION

Before-Mission and *After-Mission* pictures of the seventy in the text would be very different. *Before*, I see nervous looks, faint attempts at smiles, like students before a big exam or individuals getting ready to go on a blind date or people moments before starting on a new job. *After*, they are laughing all over themselves. Somehow, they were able to experience joy on the job.

JOY IN LEARNING

Part of their joy was in learning new things—growing, exploring, and expanding.

- They learned how to live by faith.
- They learned how to receive the hospitality of others.

- They learned how to preach, teach, and heal.
- They learned how to handle rejection and criticism.

WHAT NEW THINGS ARE YOU LEARNING THAT YOUR JOY MIGHT BE FULL?

- What do you want to learn?
- How will you ensure that you will learn it?

Considerations and Resources

- Explore the connections between play, learning, and joy.
- Read Ellen Langer's *Mindfulness* (Reading, Mass.: Addison-Wesley Publishing Company, 1989).
- Think about what it means to cultivate anticipation for new learning.
- If you don't have one, create a church library. If you do have one, begin working on plans to make it one of the brightest, most exciting areas in your church building.

My Thoughts and Ideas

_____

_____

_____

_____

_____

The *Even If* of God

Teresa Fry Brown

Text
Daniel 3:16-18 (NIV)

Theme
To celebrate faithfulness, especially when God seems absent.

Sermon Outline
THE POWER OF GOD

Lyrics to the song "God Specializes" delineate the power of God in seemingly untenable situations. Lift up current events particular to the congregation interspersed with lines from the song or other contemporary lyrics or poetry.

MEANING

Define *even*, *eventuality*, and *if*, and explore possible textual implications.

ROLES

Outline the setting of the text and roles of the main characters: Hananiah, Mishael, Azariah, Belteshazzar, and King Nebuchadnezzar.
* Why were these three young men singled out?
* What happens when assimilation is forced or heritage denied?
* Why did King Nebuchadnezzar decide to place the sixty-cubit statue in the middle of the Plain of Dura? What modern-day human idols have been erected?

• What happens when leadership is placated by followers or buys favors?

• Offer modern-day examples of poor or oppressive government, laws, rules, or regulations in families, small groups, church, community, country, or world.

RESOLVE

• What options are available during a faith crisis?

• How does one know God is present, active, or listening to the faithful?

• Under a threat of death, what does *trust* mean *even if* God answers faithful prayer differently than the person believes or anticipates God will answer?

RESCUE

• Was faith demonstrated in entering the furnace or leaving it?

• Describe the furnace and level of proposed punishment.

• Why did the king check on the furnace?

• Share companion texts regarding rescue—Psalm 91:11-13; Isaiah 43:1b-2

• How does God empower us to remain steadfast when all around us seems to be shifting during the *even if* time?

• What are examples of *even if* times?

REWARD

• How and when does God reward faithfulness?

• Offer an *Even If* Assurance Plan: Revelation 3:8-12

Considerations and Resources

• Research the Hebrew names of the Israelites. The renamed Shadrach, Meshach, Abednego, and Daniel are essential to understanding their faith and the penalty for not bowing to the idol.

- Although a staple in traditional black preaching, this text contains an infinite number of fresh entry points, particularly in grammatical structure and intent of the background characters.
- Examine local churches, architecture, icons, and memorials for items/people/locations that are revered. Use the information for modern-day examples of the king's behavior.

My Thoughts and Ideas

_____

_____

_____

_____

_____

Week Two

One More Night with the Frogs

Kirk Byron Jones

Text

Exodus 8:1-10

Theme

To confront our capacity to become comfortable with harmful behaviors and choices.

Sermon Outline

MAYBE GOD IS TRYING TO TELL YOU SOMETHING

The film *The Color Purple* ends with a rousing song entitled "Maybe God Is Trying to Tell You Something." In our story, God is trying to tell a head of state something. God is trying to convince Pharaoh to sign an emancipation proclamation and release his slaves. Pharaoh objects to the suggestion from this alien divinity and becomes indignant. He is possessed by a *defiant royal consciousness* rooted in pride and is resolved to hold the Hebrews captive.

In his book *The Prophetic Imagination* (Philadelphia: Fortress Press, 1978), Walter Brueggemann identifies three features of a royal consciousness still around today:

- An economics of affluence in which we are so well off that pain is not noticed.

- The politics of oppression in which the cries of [the least and the last] are not heard
- A religion of [easy accessibility], in which we basically create God in our own image.

Is the defiant royal consciousness still around? What kind of foreign policy might it inspire?

ENTER, THE FROGS

God commissions Moses and Aaron to serve as his envoys, his ambassadors to Pharaoh, to challenge that leader's defiant royal consciousness. God's strategy is to convince Pharaoh of his wrong by manipulating entities of nature that have become a part of the Egyptian system of worship. Ancient Egyptian religion was polytheistic; they worshiped many Gods.

The second of ten plagues is a rain of frogs. All of a sudden there were frogs all over Egypt. "Here a frog, there a frog, everywhere a frog, frog." When asked when he wanted them removed, Pharaoh surprisingly responded, "Tomorrow." He is willing to spend one more night with the frogs.

OUR FROGS

Frogs end up being a nuisance for us and those we love, but we somehow find a way to keep on living with them until "tomorrow."

- A frog may be *secret sin* that has your name and number on it, and after awhile it may not be so much of a secret any longer.
- A frog may be a *memory* that has you bound, that you won't turn loose.
- A frog may be a *feud* that you are unwilling to resolve. You've grown used to just not speaking to someone.
- A frog may be a *person* who is ruining your life, and you keep letting him or her.
- A frog may be an *attitude* that you have that's just you, and you've decided that you're not going to change for anybody.
- A frog may be a *fear* that is keeping you from dreaming and "living outside the box."

We all have "hidden frogs." Hidden frogs are submerged deep in our consciousness because the pain or guilt is too heavy to bear, the responsibility too awesome to shoulder. Yet, hidden things have a way of smoldering, building up, and erupting when we least expect.

LATER FOR THE FROGS?

Tomorrow is *the great hope*. Annie, the orphan of Broadway and movie fame, sings, "The sun will come out tomorrow."

- Tomorrow is the *great presumption*.
- Tomorrow can keep frogs of fear and doubt around that we need to get rid of today.
- Tomorrow can extend a feud that can and should end today.
- Tomorrow can put off an adventure with a dream that can start today.
- Tomorrow can postpone a creative risk that God wants you to take today.
- Tomorrow can make you miss the deliverance and salvation that can be yours today.

"This is the day that the LORD has made; let us rejoice and be glad in it" (Psalm 118:24).

Considerations and Resources

- Research the subject of frogs. Use the data to make the sermon even more interesting. For example, before you begin talking about the different kind of behavioral frogs, you can list different types of actual frogs. Electronic encyclopedias such as Encarta or Encyclopedia Britannica are ideal for this.
- If you dare, bring a frog to church. Have it visible throughout the entire sermon.
- This is an ideal opportunity to bring in a child's stuffed frog toy. Identify it in a children's sermon as "a friendly frog," and not the type you will be preaching to the adults about.

<u>My Thoughts and Ideas</u>

God's Will for You

Portia Wills Lee

Text

Philippians 4:4-7; 1 Thessalonians 5:16-18

Theme

To establish a basic spiritual philosophy for living based on God's fundamental desire for our lives.

Sermon Outline

GOD'S WILL?

Young and old alike are sometimes puzzled about the will of God. Jesus said, "It is not the will of your Father . . . that one of these little ones should perish" (Matthew 18:14 KJV), but then what? In this letter to the Christian church, Paul gives final instructions, "Rejoice evermore. Pray without ceasing. In every thing give thanks" (1 Thessalonians 5:16-18 KJV).

IN ALL CIRCUMSTANCES

- Rejoice.
- Pray.
- Praise and give thanks.

CHRIST: OUR PREEMINENT EXAMPLE

- He was tried and proved true.
- He exudes and offers abundant life.

There are many things about God that we may not understand. But God wills us to live wisely and to be secure in our relationship with God. And if we continue to do this, God offers us abundant life.

Considerations and Resources

• Summarize your basic understanding of God's will for human existence. How does it compare with the views expressed in the foregoing outline?

• Consult *The Purpose-Driven Life* by Rick Warren (Grand Rapids, Mich.: Zondervan, 2002).

• How can you preach about God's will in a way that is more buoyant and less burdensome?

• What have been your biggest struggles in discerning God's will for your life? Seek to incorporate your learning in this sermon.

My Thoughts and Ideas

_____

_____

_____

_____

_____

Week Three

When We Can't Find the Words

Kirk Byron Jones

Text

Matthew 27:67; Mark 15:48; Luke 23:57; John 19:43

Theme

To attend to the lessons of the *Wordless Texts* of Scripture.

Sermon Outline

WHEN THERE IS NOTHING THAT CAN BE SAID

You won't find the listed verses in Scripture. These are the four texts where there are no words. In my imagination, I can see a few of those first-century followers simply waving their hands. There are no words. They cannot speak their

- disappointment
- disillusionment
- doubt
- anger and grief at the sudden death of Jesus

There are no words.

Speech often takes a vacation in times of emotional extremes; in times of expansive joy, grinding anger, and gut-wrenching grief.

The writer/preacher Fredrick Buechner tells us that we need to pay more careful attention to the texts of life and Scripture that have no words. He writes in *Telling the Truth: The Gospel As Tragedy, Comedy and Fairy Tale*, "Before the Gospel is a word, it is a silence, a kind of presenting of life itself so that we see it not for what at various times we call it—meaningless or meaningful, absurd, beautiful—but for what it truly is in all its complexity, simplicity, mystery" ([San Francisco: Harper & Row, 1977], 25).

WORDLESS TEXTS

Wordless texts in life are places where we can experience not what we say, think, or hope life is; but what life really is. The four wordless texts of Scripture are significant because of what life really is in the moment. In the moment of the texts, life may be other things as well, but for sure

- it is dismay
- it is doubt
- it is frustration
- it is fear

Have you ever been there? Thank God for a faith that grants admission to such things!

On Christmas Eve 1967, Martin Luther King Jr. spoke to his congregation at Ebenezer in Atlanta and said: "I must confess to you today that not long after talking about the dream (in Washington) I started seeing it turn into a nightmare. I remember the first time I saw that dream turn into a nightmare, just a few weeks after I had talked about it. It was when four beautiful, unoffending, innocent Negro girls were murdered in a church in Birmingham, Alabama" (Martin Luther King, Jr., "A Christmas Sermon on Peace," *The Trumpet of Conscience* [San Francisco: HarperSanFrancisco], 76).

Wordless texts give us room, provide space for us to express our feelings about the nightmares of life.

As I watch, with you, on the banks, on the brink of a great Nightmare in Iraq, as I grieve our nation's warring rhetoric and rehearsals, I need a place.

- I need a place for my dismay.
- I need a place for my frustration.
- I need a place for my fear.

- I need a place for my rage.
- I need a text with no words.

CHURCH METERS

In the bayou land of Louisiana, in Mount Hermon Baptist Church, I grew up hearing and singing fast songs, slow songs, spirituals, hymns, and meters. A meter is a song of few words and lines that is spoken, hummed, and sung at the same time. A meter could break out at any time, after a fast song, after the sermon, but was usually sung during morning devotionals and testimony time when individuals took a few moments and sometimes longer to talk about what the Lord had done for them. One meter went:

> It's just like fire shut up in my bones—
> It's just like fire shut up in my bones
> I wouldn't take nothing for my journey now
> I wouldn't take nothing for my journey now
> If I couldn't say a word, I'd just wave my hand—
> If I couldn't say a word—
> > "If I Can't Say a Word . . ."
> (*Sing the following*)

> If I can't say a word . . . I'd just wave . . .

(Extended Pause, then UP FROM THE SILENCE, Sing the following)

> Are you talking about Jesus, He's a friend of mine
> Are you talking about Jesus, He's a friend of mine

Considerations and Resources

- Read *When God Is Silent* by Barabara Brown Taylor (Cambridge, Mass.: Cowley P ublications, 1988).
- Listen to Billie Holiday or another singer sing the Blues.
- Recall your bouts of wandering and wondering amid the silent moments of your faith experience.

<u>My Thoughts and Ideas</u>

_____

_____

_____

_____

_____

Say It Isn't So

Charles Henry

Text

Luke 10:25-37

Theme

To honor the truth in words we don't expect or want to hear.

Sermon Outline

A Song and a Question

In the song "Say It Isn't So," the singer wishes that things were not the way he already knows they are.

The parable of the good Samaritan reminds me of that song, not so much for the parable itself, but for the question that prompted it. "What shall I do to inherit eternal life?" seemed innocent on the surface, but Jesus recognized it for the trick that it was. The lawyer knew the laws and the requirements. It was his hope that Christ would make a mistake by responding with an answer other than the standard Old Testament truth.

The Answer

Jesus' answer left no question as to who had an opportunity to be a neighbor to the person in need.
- Opportunity is defined by proximity.
- Opportunity is defined by capacity.
- Opportunity is defined by our timing.

The answer left no question as to who was neighbor to the man. The lawyer knew it was the person who exhibited mercy. The lawyer was challenged to *practice* loving action, not just *ponder* it.

Considerations and Resources

• Research the song "Say It Isn't So" and listen to it as sung by Frank Sinatra or another artist.

• The subject of the sermon is caught in the net of his own questioning. This sermon suggests that he was somewhat troubled by Jesus' challenge-filled answer. Could it be that the subject celebrated the answer? If so, how would you preach this sermon in a different way?

• What of Jesus' other teachings might solicit a "say it isn't so" response?

My Thoughts and Ideas

_____

_____

_____

_____

_____

Week Four

Stand Up; Sit Down; Move On

Kirk Byron Jones

Text

Luke 4:16-30

Theme

To interpret and offer strategies for living with God's anointing.

Sermon Outline

JESUS COMES HOME TO TEACH

Draw a comparison between Jesus' teaching experience and the dialogical preaching tradition of the African American church. Early on, Jesus seems to be doing well; the congregation affirms him with hearty "Amens!" But not long into his presentation, "the church goes silent on him." Before long, he hears the most troubling words you can hear, "Help him, Lord." In a short span of time, Jesus goes from triumph to trouble.

WHY DID JESUS' TEACHING TAKE A SURPRISING TURN FOR THE WORSE?

Blame Jesus?

In what sense does Jesus, through his rhetoric, seem to be picking a fight?

Blame the listeners?

On the one hand, the Scripture does not offer tangible evidence that they said something to provoke Jesus. On the other hand, do people have to "say" things to get to us?

Blame the anointing?

Was Jesus merely repeating Isaiah when he said, "The Spirit of the Lord is upon me"? If the Spirit was actually on him, there is another candidate for blame: Holy Spirit Anointing.

In his book, *The Holy Spirit and Preaching*, James Forbes defines the anointing as "the experience of the presence of God" (Nashville: Abingdon Press, 1989). Perhaps the surprising tension of that day was stirred by the Spirit.

THREE STRATEGIES FOR LIVING WITH THE RISKY AND SURPRISING TENSION OF HOLY ANOINTING

Stand in the anointing.

In verse 16, Jesus "stood up." To stand in the anointing is to be who we are in the anointing. Spirituality is not about human diminishment but human enhancement.

Sit in the anointing.

In verse 20, Jesus "sat down." Sitting down is a metaphor for being still in the anointing. The anointing is replenished in stillness.

Move on in the anointing.

In verse 30, Jesus "went on his way." To go on our way is to journey on, to persevere through it all, come what may.

Considerations and Resources

• Illustrations for this sermon should be brief so as to not overshadow the pivotal story of the text. Listeners ought to feel "in" the textual story throughout the sermon to conclusion.

- Reveal the strategies one at a time. Don't list them all and go back and discuss each. You may want to cloak the strategies even more by not announcing or printing the sermon title. Anticipation and curiosity are two unsung friends of preaching.
- Read Forbes' *The Holy Spirit and Preaching* and other discussions of anointing from various perspectives.
- How do you experience anointing? What do you believe to be the strengths and challenges associated with anointed living?
- Usable Quote: On the element of holy surprise introduced above:

> What surprises there are! We are such planners! We decide how God must come into human affairs . . . While we wait at the airport, as it were, with a representative committee of dignitaries and an escort, waiting for the coming, God has a way of quietly arriving at the bus station, walking up a side street, and slipping, unnoticed, through the servant's entrance. (Gene Bartlett, *Postscript to Preaching: After Forty Years, How Will I Preach Today?* [Valley Forge, Pa.: Judson Press, 1981], 80)

My Thoughts and Ideas

_____

_____

_____

_____

_____

Then Say So

Teresa Fry Brown

Text

Psalm 107

Theme

To encourage praising God.

Sermon Outline

HARDSHIP TO HALLELUJAHS

The psalm is written in perfect verse/chorus format. One can almost hear the singing. The tension is hardship to hallelujahs.

- What are the divisions or chorus refrain markers?
- When and where was this psalm used in worship?
- Why sing praises to God?
- What hinders praise or lifting our voices?

SITUATION, SOLUTION, AND SOUND

- Progressing through the psalm, identify what hardships are encountered? By whom?
- What is God's action or intervention?
- What is the commanded response?

THE GREAT THANKSGIVING

- What are the mighty acts of God? Compare to Luke 1:46.
- Compare to the events of Revelation 7:7-9.
- What happens when one has full voice and the freedom to praise God?

Considerations and Resources

• Consult a medical dictionary, science website, or speech-language pathologist regarding voice production and what impedes voice.

• Review LeRoy Aden and Robert Hughes's, *Preaching God's Compassion: Comforting Those Who Suffer* (Minneapolis: Fortress Press, 2002).

• If necessary, talk with the music director regarding the form of the psalm and possible parallel contemporary song.

• End with a song of thanksgiving.

My Thoughts and Ideas

_____

_____

_____

_____

_____

Week Five

Unmasking the Real Enemies

Kirk Byron Jones

Text

Ephesians 6:12

Theme

To promote eradicating the attitudes and beliefs that lead to personal and social oppression.

Sermon Outline

"I WANT TO CHANGE THE SYSTEM"

Some time ago, a man standing with his daughter tried to hail a taxi in New York City. Five taxis, all with their roof lights on indicating that they were empty and on duty, passed them by. The man happened to be Danny Glover, a well-known actor, who happens to be African American. Seething at the blatant display of racist behavior, Glover called a news conference, and now the matter has sparked debate and discussion about a practice that has gone on in New York and other cities for some time. Notably, Glover did not file a complaint against the cabdrivers. He said, "I don't want to punish individual drivers, I want to change the system."

LESSONS FROM PAUL

Paul, writing to early Christians who faced discrimination and physical abuse at the hands of an increasingly hostile Roman ruling authority, sought to unmask for those first followers who the real enemies were.

The first thing Paul does is eliminate all *persons* from the "enemy list." Now if you're an early Christian at First Church of Ephesus reading this, Paul has just troubled your mental waters big time. What do you mean we don't wrestle against flesh and blood?

- What about those mean and abusive Roman soldiers? Who can ever forget what they did to Jesus?

- What about those hypocritical, lying, and conniving tax collectors who plunge their own people into deeper poverty through their common crime of demanding more tax monies than are actually due?

- What about those jail guards who beat Christians again and again, before and during their imprisonment? My God, Paul, you should know better then to write something like this, *you're in prison right now!* What do you mean we don't wrestle against flesh and blood? Of course we do. Are you mad?

- Do you think Paul is mad? What are our feelings about people who are mean and show us harm? Persons "flesh and blood" are not the real enemy. Just the opposite is closer to the truth.

- There is a Jewish teaching that yields this: "If we could see each other as we truly are, we would kneel before each other in adoration and worship."

- Luke 17:21 records Jesus putting it this way, "The kingdom of God is within you" (KJV).

WHO ARE THE REAL ENEMIES?

- The real enemies are supernatural forces that are alive *without* our help. Given the nature of some of our crimes against one another, it is not a big leap of faith to believe that we have help in our evil from outside of us.

- The real enemies are supernatural forces, insidious and prevailing, almost seeming to have a life of their own, that are alive precisely because we create them and we feed them. Such enemies include the following: apathy, ignorance, closed-mindedness, and selfishness.

A Prayer

God, we confess our intended and unintended partnership with the principalities and powers that seek to obstruct you, those that are beyond us, and those that are because of us. Empower us with the sanctified counterforces that trumpet your will and way with us. We start by saying yes afresh and anew to the astonishing and attainable principalities and powers of dialogue, diversity, unity, acceptance, and courage. Amen.

Considerations and Resources

- Consult newspapers and periodicals for incidents similar to the one identified at the beginning of this sermon.
- Read or survey *Race Matters* by Cornel West (Boston: Beacon Press, 1993).
- Reflect on your own personal experiences with oppression.
- Develop strategies for distinguishing between persons and attitudes and beliefs. Is drawing such a distinction really possible?

My Thoughts and Ideas

_____

_____

_____

_____

_____

We Wrestle

Kirk Byron Jones

Text

Genesis 32:24; Ephesians 6:12

Theme

To encourage spiritual fortitude and strength.

Sermon Outline

IN SPORT

Paul has in mind the athletic event of its day. Indeed, origins of the sport of wrestling can be traced back fifteen thousand years through depictions in cave drawings in France. The wrestling that Paul knew—what we now refer to as Greco-Roman wrestling—held a prominent place in Rome and Greece in life, legend, and literature. The distinctive feature of Greco-Roman wresting, still practiced throughout the world today, is that contestants must apply all holds above the waist. The use of legs in an offensive or defensive way is prohibited.

In this kind of wrestling, *strength* is more important than *speed*, and *endurance* is more important than *agility*. This is the kind of wrestling going on in Genesis 32:24.

IN LIFE

We can't avoid wrestling with life challenges, decisions, and changes.

- Accept that life has its hard places.
- Accept the learning in the hard places.
- Accept the growth in the hard places—the greater the challenge, the greater the growth.

God Is with Us

We do not wrestle alone; God is with us. As "Mother Pollard" assured Martin Luther King Jr. one evening, "I done told you we is with you all the way. But even if we ain't with you, God's gonna take care of you" (Taylor Branch, *Parting the Waters: America in the King Years, 1954–63* [New York: Simon & Schuster, 1988], 164.)

Considerations and Resources

• Reflect on the challenge of preaching about the reality of struggle without over-romanticizing suffering. Some people cannot experience the peaceful rest of the faith, because they have an over-fixation on the *fight* of faith.

• You might win some listeners by being able to name popular wrestlers associated with the World Wrestling Federation. Although this brand of wrestling is for the most part a sham, don't underestimate the power of starting where people are when it comes to effective communication.

• Reflect on some of your biggest struggles. Don't fail to draw from the wells of your own personal experience.

• Consider developing a sermon or Bible study series in which you teach people *how* to wrestle.

My Thoughts and Ideas

_____

_____

_____

_____

_____

OCTOBER

ARTICLE

Reflections on the Million Man March, African Americans, and the World

Gilbert H. Caldwell

It is important to remember that the Million Man March, despite the criticism before and after it, was an event that had significance that will be evident for years to come. The gathering of a million men of African descent, called together by Minister Louis Farrakhan of the Nation of Islam, had meaning that transcended those of us who gathered and the person who called for the march. Regardless of one's spiritual perspectives, there was a "Spirit" at work, some of us would say emanating from a Creator God, others might say the Spirit came from the cumulative experiences of those of the African Diaspora in America who lived, survived, and thrived, despite the dehumanization and death that others imposed upon them. Seeking to unravel the nature of the spiritual experience of the Million Man March will fascinate historians. But others of us will allow the "shock and awe" of the experience to suffice as it motivates us in all that we do.

African American persons, regardless of how many other racial/ethnic realities we possess in our DNA, no matter how "integrated" we believe ourselves to be in the larger community, nor how much energy we have expended in distancing ourselves from black history and heritage, are challenged to embrace the distinctives of the African American experience. Each one of us must be unashamed of being a "race man or woman," not for separatist reasons, or to "put down" or "dis" others, but in order to "bring to the human table" the uniqueness of our history, culture, and perspective. The nation and the world need us more than they have ever needed us before!

First, we must retrieve and reestablish in our practice that slogan I first heard uttered by the Congressional Black Caucus: "There is no permanent friend, there is no permanent enemy. There is only permanent interest." We too often "adopt" the documents and practices of others rather than "adapt" them to our interests and understandings. Whether the document is the Bible, the Constitution, the Bill of Rights, or the platforms of the Democratic and Republican parties, our experiences and the insights derived from those experiences, if taken seriously, allow us to deepen and expand the inclusive meaning of those texts. Our slave ancestors did not "adopt" a literal interpretation of Scripture that was responsible for undergirding their enslavement and segregation. They embraced Scripture as a living instrument of God's desire for them to be free. Paul's "slaves be obedient to your masters" was dismissed as being out of sync with the *totality* of Scripture. Neither the religious or political right nor the left can claim complete loyalty from us or dictate how we "practice what we preach."

Second, African American persons and communities must "learn how to fight" in ways that are constructive rather than destructive. Even as we disagree, this is a time for us to model a "blending" of the rainbow of ideas and perspectives existing among us.

When I was a boy on public school yards in North Carolina and Texas, we used to say, "He or she doesn't know how to fight." We meant that some of our colleagues fought in unfair ways that sought to destroy their opponents whom they would have to sit next to in class the next day.

Think of the "fights" between black liberals and conservatives, Democrats and Republicans, folk with Ph.D.s and those with no "Ds." I offer a short list of our "fights"; some one-way, others two-way. The recent "public" fights between some leaders and the black homosexual community is another illustration of what I mean. Another is the emerging fight between black mega-church pastors and those of us who are not pastors over mega-churches.

Before the Million Man March, a few African American women were visible and vocal in their opposition to the March. Some black men, as an elementary school classmate said years ago, "had babies with straw hats on" (Don't ask me what that means) when African American women writers spoke "truth" in their writings about the behavior of some black men. The verbal attacks on Louis Farrakhan from within the African American community depicted us as being less than our best. One of the arguments issued from some black pulpits against the MMM was, Farrakhan dominated rather than the March dominating. The verbal attacks against Bob Johnson, who founded and then sold the BET network, have not always been realistic or fair. Certainly many of us find fault in some of BET's programming before the sale and now, but we must learn the art of creative and constructive disagreement rather than that which is destructive. The list could go on and on.

Years ago I heard this proverb attributed to the wisdom resident on the continent of Africa: "When elephants fight, only the grass suffers." We have, we do, and we will disagree! Most of those who engage in public "black-on-black" attacks have the support of their constituencies, and thus they engage in open warfare without much regard for how the African American community ("the grass") may suffer. But there are still some luxuries that even the "nouveau riche" (in finances and public acclaim) African American community cannot afford. So "let's get busy," as talk show host Arsenio Hall used to say, in "blending" rather than destroying the multiplicity of our resources. What are those resources?

An illustration from the Bible (Exodus 4:1-5) is helpful. Moses is uncertain and a bit frightened about God's expectation that he become, with God's help, the liberator of his people. He lets God know this.

God's response: "What is that in your hand?"

Moses responds: "A staff."

God: "Throw it on the ground."

Moses does, and the staff becomes a snake and then becomes a staff again. Moses' experience of discovering what God can do with a staff in his hand helped him realize that he was not alone, because the God of his ancestors—Abraham, Isaac and Jacob—was with him.

African Americans "have in their hands" a history, a heritage, and a hope. The nation and the world would do well to sit at our feet and behold, grasp, and internalize that hope. We have seen the world and the nation "from the bottom up." We know through experience that the view from above and/or outside democracy, religion, ethics, value systems, integrity, civility, civilization, and culture is not the only or best view. We have seen and see the rust, the deterioration, the shortcuts in construction, and the belief that "some are more equal than others" that can only be seen from below. In this time when the religion of Islam is being "discovered" by the United States and by much of the west, the African continent and African American communities in the United States have long been aware of, have known, and have interacted with sisters and brothers of the Islamic faith. We have not been surprised that some within Islam have called into question cultural arrogance, racism, colonialism, and the contradictions of our practices of religious and cultural pluralism.

Those of us who are ministers in Christian churches, whether our denomination is historically black or white, have felt and often appreciated the ever-present Jury among us represented by the Nation of Islam and orthodox Islam. They have reminded us that the cross in our churches too often became the burning cross of the Ku Klux Klan that served as a symbol of those who would destroy the principles we have claimed to profess and practice. We have so much of universal benefit to share with the nation and the world, if we believed in what we have in our hands.

Finally, we must reclaim and then share with the world our ability to embrace and be liberated by our profound understandings of *Soul*. Our ancestors took the leftovers and the leavings from the kitchen and created soul food, now a universal delicacy. We brought the exuberance, confidence, and bodaciousness of Soul to music, dance, literature, athletics, education, boardrooms, pulpits, theaters, movie screens, and elected offices. Certainly "the world needs love," but it also needs Soul. A million men on a warm October 16, 1995, gathered in Washington, not just for ourselves, or for those who look like us, but for all of human creation. African American, Black, Negro, Colored (or whatever designation is used) men gathered to gain strength to be "Wounded Healers," not just for ourselves and our communities, but for the world. My hope is that all who read my words will be allowed to speak as a fellow citizen of the world.

October

SERMON OUTLINES

Radical, Revolutionary Stewardship

Cheryl Kirk-Duggan

Text

Genesis 1:26-31

Theme

Because we are given dominion over the earth, God calls us to be radical, revolutionary stewards. Stewardship concerns the use of all resources given to us in trust by God. This involves the right use of power as we accord sacred worth to ourselves, others, and nature.

Sermon Outline

TO LIVE IN LOVING RELATIONSHIP WITH GOD MEANS TO HAVE A RADICAL, REVOLUTIONARY RELATIONSHIP OF STEWARDSHIP WITH OUR BODIES, MINDS, AND SPIRITS

- God created us for ultimate intimacy—out of love—to think, to grow, to learn, to be, and to share.
- In the first creation story, God speaks; something exists; God calls that thing good. On the sixth day, God spoke human beings into existence and called us good: this includes sexuality.

- To function in a balanced, loving capacity requires that we know who we are: sacred beings that live in a sacred world.
- Stewardship of bodies, minds, and spirits means a commitment to a healthy lifestyle. We need to understand how to use our bodies; how to strengthen our minds; how to gird up our spirits: how to eat, exercise, think, pray, meditate, and discern.
- Violence through language and physical or psychological force is unacceptable.

To Live in the World as a Faithful Being Means to Have a Radical, Revolutionary Relationship of Stewardship with Our Time

- Where and how we spend our time tells what is important to us.
- We are called to value ourselves and value our time.
- Each of us has a call on our lives for some form of ministry; these ministries require an investment of time.
- We are *Ecclesiastes people:* "For everything there is a season" (Ecclesiastes 3:1).
- Spending too much time on any one thing in any one place is unhealthy.

To Live in the World in Love with Ourselves and Our Neighbors Requires That We Have a Radical, Revolutionary Relationship of Stewardship with Our Finances

- Money is not good or bad; it just is. Money is a medium of exchange for goods or services rendered.
- Too many of us have mastered the art of consumerism. We make poor choices when it comes to spending and saving money.
- We must also get the money we are entitled to for the jobs we do; a servant and a worker is worthy of his or her hire.

- Our entire home and family budget needs to be set up as a tithing system.
- Money is not separate and apart from who we are or what we do; how we spend our money says a lot about what we really value in life.

Considerations and Resources

- What would you consider to be the most radical dimensions of stewardship expressed in this sermon? What radical ideas would you think of adding?
- How does the sermon's understanding of stewardship differ from traditional understandings of stewardship?
- It is possible to preach a message on each of the three main sections of the sermon. Consider developing this sermon into a three-part sermon or Bible study series on stewardship.
- www.timedaytime.org: This is the website of a national movement to promote a greater balance between labor and leisure. October 24 is "Take Back Your Time" day.
- *Affluenza: The All-Consuming Epidemic*, edited by John De Graaf, David Wann, and Thomas H. Naylor (San Francisco: Berrett-Koehler Publishers, 2001). This book is one of the most informative and provocative discussions of consumerism in the United States.

My Thoughts and Ideas

_____

_____

_____

_____

_____

Commissioned to Stewardship

Portia Wills Lee

Text

Acts 16:11-15

Theme

Through observing the dimensions, we may practice good stewardship in gratitude to God.

Sermon Outline

GOD'S CALL

God calls each of us to do great things in the name of Jesus. Jesus offers us life and life more abundantly. When we learn to live our lives in faith and not fear, we come to understand that God has already commissioned us to do powerful work in the name of Jesus. Throughout the Bible, we find powerful women who moved beyond their limitations to greatness. Look at Moses' wife and Hagar, Esther, Ruth, Mother Mary, and the sister at the well. Look at sisters in our "her-story": Sojourner Truth, Harriett Tubman, Jarena Lee, Fannie Lou Hamer, Rosa Parks, Wilma Rudolph, and Marilyn D. Wills, to name a few.

COMMISSIONED TO BE STEWARDS

- Lydia was a businesswoman from Tytira, a purple cloth designer.
- We are called to handle business in the world and in the church.
- We are called to be good stewards over our own bodies.

- In 1 Corinthians 3:16-17, Paul writes "Do you not know that you are God's temple and that God's Spirit dwells in you? . . . For God's temple is holy, and you are that temple."
- We may take care of ourselves through fasting and praying and exercising and eating healthy.
- We are called to be stewards over our finances.

COMMISSIONED TO SERVE

- Not only was Lydia baptized, but also she ensured that her household was baptized.
- Her relationship with God and understanding of being a good steward gave her a desire to serve others.

Considerations and Resources

- Consult stewardship manuals as prepared by your denomination.
- Study the meaning of stewardship. Craft ways of speaking on this subject that are inviting and stimulating.
- Consult with congregants prior to preaching this message. Specifically discuss ways to make this perennial "thorn topic" in the church a point of heightened interest and celebration.

My Thoughts and Ideas

_____

_____

_____

_____

_____

Welcome Home

Teresa Fry Brown

Text

Psalm 84:1-2, 10; Revelation 21:1-3

Theme

To recognize and honor genuine hospitality and service in the church.

Sermon Outline

BEAUTIFUL HOME

Television and movie story lines historically present comedic or dramatic representations of "home" situations. These "true-to-life" situations are useful examples of "lovely dwelling" places and their antithesis. The proliferation of "home improvement" shows such as *Trading Spaces* or *While You Were Out* purport that with a little fix-up, home life is beautiful and welcoming. The focus texts suggest a permanence of a "beautiful home," where the welcome mat is always out.

TYPES OF HOMES

Describe the types of homes located in the biblical and in the congregational experience: location, size, shape, composition, neighborhood, activities, and occupants.

- What security measures usher one into the home or bar entrance?
- Explore both the function and the real experience of church ushers.

Focus Text (Psalm 84:1-9)

- When was this text used in worship?
- Why was the songwriter grieving?
- Walk through each verse and look for parallels in contemporary worship and home life.
- Attend to major concepts of comfort, nourishment, and hospitality.
- Consider the history of the Black Church. How does it feel to be barred from worship?
- Are there spirituals, hymns, or testimonies in slave narratives that speak to a longing to worship God?
- After an extended absence, how does it feel to finally arrive at home? Listen to Stephanie Mills's song "Home" or other songs about home.

Central Focus of Occasion (Verses 10-12)

- Read from *The Message* or other paraphrase translations. Write your own focusing on the elation of entering God's house and serving as a greeter.
- Why serve as an usher?
- Benefits and "blowups" of service.
- How does God (the supreme doorkeeper/usher) welcome the faithful?
- See Revelation 21 for a description of the welcome to final home.
- Use sensory information to develop a description of the home into which God welcomes the faithful.

Considerations and Resources

• Consult Cheryl Kirk-Duggan, *African American Special Days* (Nashville: Abingdon Press, 1996).

• Consider the lyrics to "Soon and Very Soon" by Andraé Crouch or "When We Get Over There" by Hezekiah Walker. These are poignant songs about receipt of the ultimate reward.

• Consult denominational publications on the duties of ushers.

• Survey your congregation regarding how hospitality is understood and practiced in the home, on the job, and in the church.

My Thoughts and Ideas

_____

_____

_____

_____

_____

Worship at the River

Portia Wills Lee

Text

Acts 16:11-15

Theme

To celebrate the refreshing, healing waters of worship.

Sermon Outline

LYDIA STYLE WORSHIP

- Lydia is believed to have been a Gentile who converted to Judaism.
  - God opened her heart; she listened and responded.
  - In Philippi, she gathered with the other women at the river to worship.
  - We should love worshiping God in praise because when the praises go up, the blessings come down.

RIVER WORSHIP

- There are times when we must steal away to the river (a place of serenity) to become energized by the quiet presence of God.
  - The slave castles in Ghana are located on the oceanfront.
  - The waters gave people relief from the heat and ground.
  - The waters empowered and energized.
  - Our ancestors continued to find strength as slaves in this country by gathering at the river to worship God.
  - Our baptism in the water reminds us of going under the water and coming up empowered by God.

Considerations and Resources

- Think about the spirituality of water. Why do you think water remains a powerful spiritual symbol?
- Research the song, "Shall We Gather at the River" by Robert Lowry.
- Visit and speak with someone who spends a great deal of time on water. What is his or her testimony about the river?
- Consider your own experience with water. How can your experience influence the sermon?
- Prepare a portion, if not all, of the sermon near a body of water.

My Thoughts and Ideas

_____

_____

_____

_____

_____

Week Three

Now

Teresa Fry Brown

Text

Jude 17-25

Theme

To understand the seriousness of discipleship responsibilities.

Sermon Outline

DISCIPLESHIP RESPONSIBILITY

Christian responsibility at times is viewed as what is expedient, distant, or agenda-oriented. The text focuses on the necessity of immediate action.

• What current events (individual, church, national, or global) demand immediate attention, address, and action rather than further discussion?

• What are Jesus' commands on the lives of disciples?

• When is "now"? Explore the definition and application of the term.

BACKGROUND OF BOOK OF JUDE

• Explore authorship, culture, and importance to church doctrine.

• The book mentions intruders in the church. Are there examples of people, places, or things that interfere with the work and mission of the church?

- The constant presence of false teachers may lead people to think faithfulness is useless.
- How would you reassure them that victories are sometimes small but the ultimate victory over evil is worth the journey?

CORE DISCIPLESHIP VERSES (17-23)

- The text gives three instructions for each disciple. They are prerequisites of receipt of the promise. They seem costly. An effective treatment of the charge will fully exegete each proposition with supportive information and must be interpreted ethically rather than given cursory one-sentence treatment.
- Ancient texts such as Syriac are instructive on repentance.

NOW

Verse 24 begins with the word *now*. This provides a point of departure for celebration. This doxology is widely used in black churches at the end of worship. The salvation plan of Jesus is presented in the last two verses.

Considerations and Resources

- A thesaurus and good dictionary are beneficial when preparing a sermon using lesser parts of speech: adverbs, adjectives, conjunctions, and prepositions.
- When using a one-chapter book, carefully frame the target verse in order to sharpen the central purpose statement and to avoid a meandering or dense sermon body. Present the background of the text and textual information in the following verses in short sentences or phrases.
- Emphasize the importance of doxologies in worship and in the biblical text. Doxologies and benedictions are often viewed as a means to end a service rather than blessings connected to the text. See Gennifer Brooks, *Praise the Lord: Litanies, Prayers, and Occasional Services* (Lima, Ohio: CSS Publishing, 1996) or Linda Hollies, *Trumpet in Zion: Black Church Worship* (Cleveland, Ohio: Pilgrim Press, 2001).

• Consult a science or biology book on predators that exemplify those who seek to destroy God's work.

My Thoughts and Ideas

_____

_____

_____

_____

_____

How Can We Sing the Lord's Song in a Foreign Land?

Gilbert H. Caldwell

Text

Psalm 137:4

Theme

To hear sociopolitical truth in complex times.

Sermon Outline

FOREIGNNESS

Do we dare (I say we must) assess the "foreignness" in our practice of democracy, the foreignness in our capitalistic system, and the foreignness in some forms of Christianity we practice?

• Democracy: Ours claims are to be a government "of, by, and for the people." Does not the preacher have the responsibility of critiquing a democracy that demonstrates a glaring inability to "be" for the people? Slow response time, disorganization, poor planning—these and much more challenge the woman or man in the pulpit to encourage listeners to raise the question *why?*

• Capitalism: Historically our nation's leaders spent time and energy pointing out the flaws of communism. Now that communism is no longer the reality or the threat that it once was, is not the preacher "called" to "gently push" from the pulpit our capitalistic system that is demeaning and dehumanizing of those who have no capital?

• Christianity: Has our practice of the Christian faith become so individualistic and heavenly-centered that it is no earthly good? Has Christianity become "foreign" to the mandate of Luke 4:18? The Spirit of the Lord expects the proclamation of good news to the poor that offers not only the "bread of heaven," but also the "bread" that sustains life. Authentic Christianity is in the business of releasing captives, recovering the sight of the blind, letting the oppressed go free, and declaring "this is the year of the Lord."

WHAT IS THE LORD'S SONG?

Having now broadened the definition of "foreign land," what now is the Lord's song that must be sung?

• First, it is a "song" that the singer must have some personal acquaintance with. At times, our reluctance to "preach truth to power" is not because we are proponents of the strict separation of church and state, but because we have not allowed the "Lord's song" to empower us personally. Thus we have no personal experience of its transforming power. The preacher must know intimately the song.

• Second, the Lord's song must be sung in the midst of the signs of foreignness in democracy, capitalism, and Christianity because if the preacher will not do it, who will? Was it M.C. Hammer who used to sing/say, "Can't touch this"? We, who dare stand behind the sacred desk called the pulpit, sometimes preach to the "easy targets" and avoid the systemic topics. It is less of a challenge to preach against personal sin than against institutional and systemic sin.

• Third, the Lord's song has a special melody and words for systemic sin. Reinhold Niebuhr wrote *Moral Man and Immoral Society*. The Lord's song needs to be sung in the midst of immoral, systemically evil society.

• Fourth, the Lord's song has tucked into a bit of the overturning of the tables in the temple that we identify with Jesus. Our listeners sometimes are victimized and fall prey to the distorted democracy, crafty capitalism, and charlatan Christianity. The Lord's song tells us that we are special because God made us that way. Anything within church or society that "messes" with our God-given specialness displeases God. The

Lord's song sounds a little bit like: Ain't gonna let nobody [no faulty democracy, capitalism, or Christianity] turn us around."

If the Church of Jesus Christ does not hear a song that can be sung in the marketplace, who will do the singing? The crooked politicians, the greedy CEOs, and those few preachers who exploit the gospel? Of course not!

Considerations and Resources

• Pre-sermon considerations: Prayerful reflection before developing a different sermon in response to this verse is a necessity for the preacher who seeks to allow God to speak through her/him in this complex time. We live our lives exploring what it is, what does it sound like, do I know it when I hear it, am I able to sing it? Prayer, study, worship, service, witnessing, evangelizing—all give us opportunity to deepen our acquaintance with "the Lord's song." But in the twenty-first century, particularly after the devastation of hurricanes Katrina and Rita and what we learned about ourselves and governmental response as we and it sought to respond to those affected, we must ask a more difficult question.

• Addressing social issues in the pulpit is an honorable part of the African American preaching tradition. What are the sociopolitical dimensions of this sermon?

• Social Justice Preaching Resources:

  ○ *Preaching to the Black Middle Class: Words of Challenge, Words of Hope* by Marvin A. McMickle (Valley Forge, Pa.: Judson Press, 2000)

  ○ *In a Blaze of Glory: Womanist Spirituality as Social Witness* by Emilie Townes (Nashville: Abingdon Press, 1995)

  ○ *Preaching Liberation* by James Harris (Minneapolis: Fortress Press, 1995)

  ○ *Speaking the Truth in Love: Prophetic Preaching to a Broken World* by J. Philip Wogman (Louisville, Ky.: Westminster John Knox Press, 1998) o *Preaching Justice: Ethnic and Cultural Perspectives* by Christine Marie Smith (Cleveland, Ohio: United Church Press, 1998)

My Thoughts and Ideas

_____

_____

_____

_____

_____

Week Four

Dangerous, Healing Laughter

Cheryl Kirk-Duggan

Text

Psalm 126

Theme

To celebrate the divine call to laugh.

Sermon Outline

LAUGHTER TEXTS

- Psalm 2: God laughs at evildoers.
- Psalm 126: *Our* mouths filled with laughter.
- Genesis 18: Sarah laughs in disbelief and shame.
- Matthew 9: The crowd laughs in ridicule because they think the girl is dead and Jesus is too late.
- Ecclesiastes 2: A cynical commentary on the uselessness of human effort to change the world, reach understanding, or possess happiness.

THE PSALMS

The psalms are Israel's prayer book, an anthology or grouping of songs, poems, and prayers sung and spoken by individuals and communities in a huge variety of historical and social settings. Grouped in five books or divisions, they represent the full range of human emotions in conversation with God.

- Psalms represent the practical theology of Judaism, involving the ecstasy of praise and lament of tragedy.
- Psalms move us through stages in life.

In Memory, We Can Look Back at How God Has Delivered Us in the Past

A community that had been in bondage, in Babylonian captivity, probably sang the song of Psalm 126. When Israel and Judah fell, by 587 B.C.E., they were sent to Babylon. They were without a home, so their return would have been a dream come true.

The return to Jerusalem brought about great joy. Think of the returns in your own life: reunions, from illness, from hard times, coming back home, and for those near the end of their journey, a going home to their eternal home.

- This is a time of joy and laughter. Think about the joy of those slaves who learned of the Emancipation Proclamation.
- Think of the end of World War II, with ticker tape parades in New York City.
- Think of the workers during the civil rights movement that learned of the Montgomery Bus Boycott decision.

How Marvelous to Exercise the Gift of Laughter

Each and every day we can laugh and dance with God through prayer. To laugh means we show mirth and joy, and we chuckle with explosive sound; we make joyous sounds because we find amusement or pleasure in something; our response to all the funny things that happened; sometimes we laugh out of embarrassment.

The "danger" of laughing is that we may not take ourselves too seriously.

- The danger of laughter is that we might enjoy ourselves.
- The danger of laughter is that we might know pleasure.
- The danger of laughter is that we might no longer be victims.

- The danger of laughter is that we might really get well and healed.

Considerations and Resources

- Read resources by Walter Brueggemann, especially *The Prophetic Imagination* (Minneapolis: Fortress Press, 2001).
- James Cone writes in *Martin & Malcolm & America: A Dream or a Nightmare*, "Anger and humor are like the left and right arm. They complement each other. Anger empowers the poor to declare their uncompromising opposition to oppression, and humor keeps them from being consumed by their fury" ([Maryknoll, N.Y.: Orbis Books, 1991], 309).
- Consult *On the Real Side: Laughing, Lying, and Signifying, The Underground Tradition of African-American Humor That Transformed American Culture, from Slavery to Richard Pryor* by Mel Watkins (New York: Simon & Schuster, 1994).
- Laugh more.

My Thoughts and Ideas

_____

_____

_____

_____

The Real God

Cheryl Kirk-Duggan

Text

1 Kings 18:20-21, 30-32, 36

Theme

We are called to worship the God of Abraham and Sarah, Isaac and Rebecca, Israel/Jacob, Leah and Rachel.

Sermon Outline

PRAYER IS THE KEY TO SEEING AND LISTENING, SO THAT WE CAN KNOW GOD

• The first time I heard this text preached was in the film *A Man Called Peter*, the story of the Rev. Peter Marshall, who became the Chaplain to the U.S. Senate.

• The battle on Mount Carmel is a showdown between Baal and his worshipers, and between Yahweh and the children of Israel.

• Some of us are afflicted with the Ahab syndrome: We want what others have and are unsure of the God we serve.

MANY OF US CONSCIOUSLY AND UNCONSCIOUSLY PRACTICE IDOLATRY

We worship everything but God. We spend our time, our money, and our thoughts on various things. Our idolatry and needing to get even keep us from being healthy and embodying salvation.

281

GOD IS THE AWESOME EMBODIMENT OF LOVE

- God created us for relationship.
- God sent Jesus Christ, the incarnation of love, to teach us by example.
- As covenant people, we are called to a holy life; and Lent is a good time to begin the process.

Considerations and Resources

- The preacher begins by recalling hearing someone else preach this text. Have you heard this text preached before? Do you have a method of cataloging insights from sermons, books, sightings, and conversations?
- How do you define idolatry? What are some biblical/ theological definitions of idolatry?
- How do we know a false God when we see or have one? Create a list entitled "Ten Features of False Gods."
- Can religious realities become false gods, for example worship, prayer, and ministry?

My Thoughts and Ideas

_____

_____

_____

_____

_____

November

NOVEMBER

ARTICLE

Keeping Preaching Fresh

Kirk Byron Jones

One of my most memorable preaching experiences occurred during a revival. The experience began during the ride to the church. I was feeling worn and was grateful that Deacon Seay had offered to drive me that night. What I really needed him or any other caring soul to do for me that evening was preach. I just didn't feel like I had it in me. On top of that—and no doubt my mood had something to do with it—the sermon on Judas I had planned to preach was coming up short inside of me. Though it was a sermon I had preached faithfully and spiritually before, there seemed to be a staleness about it. Perhaps "The Bitter and the Better in All of Us" had run its preaching course, and preaching it one more time would be preaching it one time too many. I needed help fast.

Suddenly an idea graced me: What if you begin the sermon in the first person? What would happen if, instead of your preaching the sermon, you allowed Judas to preach it? Sweet interest immediately began to hear from the critic inside: "Aside from brief dialogues, you have little to no experience preaching in the person of biblical characters, preaching in first person. If you do this, you will not only be preaching in the first person, but that person will be Judas, the damned disciple. You have all of less than forty minutes to work out the necessary changes and alterations in your notes. Veto this melancholic-induced inspiration, you fool; this is no time to go off searching for sermonic freshness!"

But I couldn't shake the idea of Judas preaching. I asked Deacon Seay what he felt about the idea. His enthusiasm for it was instant and genuine. He thought people needed to hear something different. That night Judas began the sermon and took it about halfway, before I interrupted. It was a moving experience.

Not just the preaching, but the process of refashioning and refreshing a sermon was meaningful to me. One of the daunting challenges of preaching regularly in the same pulpit Sunday after Sunday is creating and re-creating interest for what you have to say. It is the task of handling and being handled by old themes in new and, ideally, adventurous ways.

One way irresponsibly to cut short reflection and discussion about this matter of freshness in the pulpit is to conclude that it is the Spirit's job to invoke interest regularly, and leave it at that. But what of our role as active and thoughtful vessels through which creative spirit flows? We have an important part to play in helping make the preaching moment a fresh one for ourselves and those who listen to us.

There are countless ways to go about doing this. **Resist habit in sermon construction.** Review some of your manuscripts and notes and determine what your tendencies are, and then seek to alter them from time to time. **Practice illustrative variety.** What pictures do you use to make your points? Do you rely heavily on personal experience? Pay more attention to the experiences of others through life observation and through reading and refer to them more in preaching.

Come home in different ways. In our tradition, we tend to conclude the sermon on the mountain of emotional release. May we continue to herald with great joy and sound. But are there different, no less fervent, ways to cross the finish line? If God soulfully communicated to Elijah with a "still small voice," is there some homiletical gold to be discovered in cultivating the small voice of preaching? This is the voice that can shout in sounds that are just above a whisper. This is the voice that can dutifully affirm the faith by daring to leave the sermon open-ended, so as to signal not the end of something, but the continuation of something: the listener's ongoing discussion with the word in the week ahead.

Finally, **never, ever get over the Story.** When it comes to preaching the gospel, beneath all worthwhile techniques, there is a wonderful Story of stories about a loving God who keeps coming after us. It is a story of divine defiance about God's bold resistance to our negligence, apathy, and, at bottom, our fear. Through it all, God keeps coming and calling. I suspect that if I ever get over this astounding truth "too good not to be true" (as Frederick Buechner phrases it), my preaching days will be over. I suspect, as well, that remaining enticed by the story helps my attempt to preach in a way that will draw the attention of my listeners, for a while at least.

Joe Williams, the great jazz singer, died in 1999 at the age of eighty. (I imagine the angels are still marveling over this new voice in heaven.) In an article in the *New York Times* ("Joe Williams, Jazz Singer of Soulfull Tone and Timing, Is Dead at 80," March 31, 1999, sec. B8), Jon Pareles wrote of an important stage in Williams's career:

> His vocal style was changing. When he began singing, he often performed without amplification, belting above the band. But during his years with the [Count] Basie band, he listened to tape recordings of his nightly performances, and he honed his style, paring away nonessentials, improving his intonation and adding new subtleties. His role with the Basie band was as a blues singer, but he was increasingly drawn to ballads.

Joe Williams never arrived; he was constantly evolving. Was this an important key to his musical longevity and genius?

Preaching freshness is maintained, most of all, through intimacy with God. Communion with God leads to a thirst for creativity and change. In the company of such powerful forces, fresh preaching is not only possible, but also inevitable.

November

SERMON OUTLINES

Week One

Fooling with Fools

Charles Henry

Text

Proverbs 13:20

Theme

To consider ways that "foolishness" makes for stunted emotional and spiritual growth.

Sermon Outline

WHO ARE FOOLS?

- Fools occupy their time and thought with trifles.
- Fools "make a mock at sin."
- Fools neglect important truths and realities.
- Fools do not prepare for great and unavoidable events.

HOW DO WE WALK WITH THEM?

- By frequenting their company.
- By following their examples.
- By reading their books.

FOOLISH CONSEQUENCES

- Vices.
- Unnecessary suffering.

Considerations and Resources

• The old saying "a rotten apple spoils the barrel" is often applied to friendships, and with good reason. Our friends and associates affect us profoundly sometimes. Gather more "folk wisdom" related to ways we can become fools.

• The fool may have hidden spiritual strengths. Can you think of any?

• What of the "sacred foolishness" of God?

• How do you balance avoiding negative foolishness while becoming "a fool for Christ"?

My Thoughts and Ideas

Keep On Pouring

Kirk Byron Jones

Text

2 Kings 4:1-7

Theme

To promote prosperity through giving.

Sermon Outline

NOTHING IN THE HOUSE

A mother, recently widowed (her husband had been a preacher of God's word), has come down to her last. The rain of food and clothing from family members and friends immediately after her husband's death has stopped. Bills are piling up. In fact, one collector has threatened her with the cruelly unthinkable: he will take her children as slaves in lieu of the bills she cannot pay. Under the law, he could do it and he would do it. Fear now compounds her grief. Her load is heavy, almost unbearable.

In her crisis, she cries out to someone who had worked with her husband side by side in ministry. The friend, Elisha, hears her plight and is filled with concern. Indeed, a sense of responsibility for his fallen comrade's family rises up inside of Elisha. He asks her two questions, back to back. First, "What can I do for you?" And then, before she has a chance to answer, with *holy urgency* he asks, "What do you have in the house?" To Elisha's back-to-back question, she sort of gives a back-to-back answer. Her first response is, "I don't have anything in the house, nothing."

A Little Oil

Often that's our first assessment of a crisis situation, "There is nothing that I can do." "There is nothing that I can think of." "Nothing can help now." But it's been my experience—and I'm sure it has been your experience as well—that when I look a little more closely, think a little more deeply, and wait a little while longer, *something* will take *nothing's* place. That's just what happened in this woman's case. Her first answer was nothing, but a moment latter, she responded, "Well I do have a jar of oil." Oil was the all-purpose substance in every household in those days, used for cooking and also for anointing and sacrifice in religious practice and for lighting lamps and for healing wounds of small children. She remembers the jar of oil, her last.

Then it really gets interesting—and I believe a little scary, at first, for the mother—because Elisha tells her to round up the kids and ask them to go around the neighborhood collecting empty containers, as many as they can find. No doubt this mother's first thought was, "What if that collector is out there, the one who has threatened to take away my children?"

Give It Away

The next thing Elisha says is somewhat frightening as well. When the containers are placed before her, she is to pour her oil in her neighbors' containers. It would appear that the prophet is suggesting that she give her last away. But to her credit and our amazement, any hesitancy or ambivalence or anxiety the mother feels about the prophet's plan quickly melts away. The most amazing thing of all was what happened as she began returning the vessels they'd collected.

It was about the fourth or fifth container when she began to notice something: though she was constantly pouring oil from her jar into the other jars, her jar was not getting any lighter. In fact, it felt just as heavy as it did when she first started pouring.

THE IN-POURING OF LOVING GRACE

The lesson is insanely clear and true, and we have lived it. Our out-pouring of self, love, labor, and finances, including the tithe, is matched and surpassed by God's in-pouring of love and grace. It is a loving grace that transcends measurement in dollars and cents. Rather, its value is in where it takes us: to the place of contentment and peace, the place of divine security.

Considerations and Resources

• This is a narrative outline that retells the story, ending with a single lesson. Identify other elements in the text that may be highlighted, leading to a different kind of sermon.

• Some people give and give to the point of exhaustion. How might you take that reality into consideration as you prepare and preach this sermon?

• Consider having a cast of congregants-turned-actors assist you in *presenting* this message.

My Thoughts and Ideas

Week Two

Running on Empty

Portia Wills Lee

Text

2 Kings 4:8

Theme

To introduce strategies for combating emotional, physical, and spiritual exhaustion.

Sermon Outline

LIVING ON "E"

There are times in all of our lives when we feel as if we are running on empty. No matter what our status is in life or what our relationship is with the Lord, we are all confronted with seasons of void, destitute, uselessness, null, and hollow.

The woman in our text had some status in her community because she was married to a prophet, which also means she had some knowledge and understanding of God. Yet she, too, is confronted with a season of running on empty. Her husband is now dead. She no longer has an income coming into her house. She can no longer provide food for her children to eat. She cannot pay her bills.

ADMIT

- Emptiness tells us we have a need.
- Identify the need.

- Authority and the power of boldness to speak God's Word.
- Healing for our fragmented souls.
- Financial blessing so we can give back to God and his people.

PRAY

- Only God can fill our emptiness.
- God will give us the vision.
- God will give us the power.
- God will give us the patience.

ACCEPT

- God wants to bless us, but oftentimes we miss our blessing because we don't want to partner with God to get our blessing.
- God blesses us through neighbors.

Considerations and Resources

- Rest.
- Read *Rest in the Storm: Self-care Strategies for Clergy and Other Caregivers* by Kirk Byron Jones (Valley Forge, Pa.: Judson Press, 2001).
- If you have been pastoring for more than seven years and have not taken an extended break, a sabbatical of at least three months, seriously consider doing so. You do yourself, your family, the church, and your ministry a tremendous injustice by continuing to "run on empty."

My Thoughts and Ideas

_____

_____

_____

_____

_____

Resolving Life's Conflicts

Charles Henry

Text

2 Corinthians 13:5-14

Theme

To examine spiritual avenues for conflict resolution.

Sermon Outline

HARMFUL CONFLICT IS A REALITY OF LIFE

Conflict is a word that needs little definition. We see conflict all around on a global scale. There is conflict in the home: marriages ending in divorce, teenagers running away from home, and young people committing suicide. The first century was not immune to conflict, and neither was the early church.

CONFLICT IN THE EARLY CHURCH

Perhaps no church experiences conflicts like the church at Corinth. Paul's first letter tells us about a split in the church that had divided the congregation into four factions. This church was one located in Corinth—a city considered the worldliest of the first century—and made conflict a part of life. There were conflicts over doctrine; there were serious questions over meat offered to idols; there were conflicts over moral behavior; there were conflicts over the celebration of the Lord's Supper. The disagreements between Paul and the church began to degenerate to a "personality dispute." They eventually challenged his apostleship and questioned his authority to teach them at all.

CONFLICT RESOLUTION IN THE CHURCH

Conflicts are resolved when we begin to examine ourselves
- instead of our brother
- in spite of our fears
- in order to see Christ

CONFLICTS ARE RESOLVED WHEN WE BEGIN TO ENCOURAGE OUR BROTHER

- with the noblest ambition
- with the sincerest integrity

CONFLICTS ARE RESOLVED WHEN WE BEGIN TO EXPRESS OUR FORGIVENESS

- in a spirit of reconciliation
- in a spirit of expectation
- in a spirit of love

Considerations and Resources

- Read *Getting to Amen: 8 Strategies for Managing Conflict in the African American Church* by Lora-Ellen McKinney (Valley Forge, Pa.: Judson Press, 2005).
- Consider the following quote from *Callings: Finding and Following an Authentic Life* by Gregg Levoy:

> Either way, the opposing forces occupy a space that is like an *ecotone*, a transition between two ecological communities like forest and grassland or river and desert. They compete, yes; the word ecotone means a house divided, a system in tension. But they also exchange, swapping juices, information, and resources. Ecotones have tremendous biological diversity and resilience. ([New York: Harmony Books, 1997], 53)

- What are some other ways to perceive and imagine conflict and tension?

My Thoughts and Ideas

Week Three

Thanksgiving Sunday

Soul Food: The Bread of Heaven

Cheryl Kirk-Duggan

Text

Matthew 6:11

Theme

To affirm that God is our ultimate and abiding source.

Sermon Outline

Textual Background

To understand this text fully, it is important to be aware of the Gospel writer's agenda. This prayer, set within the Sermon on the Mount, resonates with themes that emerge throughout Matthew: God as Creator/Abba; the coming rule or kingdom of God; doing God's will; the need for receiving divine forgiveness and practicing human forgiveness.

Biblical scholars disagree about Jesus' meaning in the Lord's Prayer. Some see it as existential, referring to present human experience on earth; others see it as eschatological, referring to God's coming rule on earth. The prayer lends itself to both interpretations, and further questions are posed by the existence of different translations and the problems inherent in the process of translation.

GOD IS OUR BREAD

My dad's byword was "God provides."

Throughout the world, people eat some form of bread. Worldwide, breads are made of corn (30 percent), wheat (27 percent), rice (27 percent), barley (8 percent), oats (2 percent), rye (1 percent), and millet and other items (5 percent). We eat yeast breads, bagels, French breads or baguettes, sourdough and sponge breads, pancakes, and waffles. Many U.S. Native American groups make a fried dough product called simply, fry bread. Southwestern Native Americans have been using colored cornmeal for centuries. Hopi women make piki bread, which is paper-thin and baked by spreading thin layers of dough on hot rocks.

Other kinds of breads include: kneel down bread, so-called because one has to kneel through much of the baking of this bread in a fire pit; cornmeal dumplings; flattened oval cornbreads; hoecakes; and shuck bread, which is wrapped in the dough in corn husks. Latino/as make flour and corn tortillas. For everyday breads, families of both central European and Scandinavian ancestry rely on commercially baked breads for the wonderful sourdough, rye, pumpernickel, crisp brotchen, flatbreads, pancakes, and waffles. Most Asians traditionally eat bread only as steamed bread or dumplings. Barbecued pork is the favorite filling. An Ethiopian pancake is a flatbread called *injera*. Black folks in this country make biscuits, corn bread, hot water corn bread, hoecakes, and rolls.

THE POWER OF "GIVE US"

- "Give us" is an imperative, a command.
- "Give us" assumes there is a God, a God who cares, a God who listens.
- "Give us" assumes assurance and trust, a relationship.

God Will Never Forsake Us
or Leave Us Alone

Daily bread may include everything that has to do with the support and needs of the body, from food, drink, clothing, shoes, house, home, land, animals, money, goods, devout spouses, children, workers, leaders, devout and faithful leaders, good government, good weather, peace, health, self-control, good reputation, good friends, faithful neighbors, and the like. The word *bread* meant those things that are necessary and simple.

The Greek word *epiousion*, the adjective that modifies "bread" in the passage, has no known parallels in Greek writing and may have meant "for tomorrow." The petition, "Give us this day our daily bread," may thus mean, "Give us today a foretaste of the heavenly banquet to come." This interpretation is supported by Ethiopic versions and by St. Jerome's reference to the reading "bread of the future" in the lost Gospel According to the Hebrews. The eschatological interpretation suggests that the Lord's Prayer may have been used in a Eucharistic setting in the early church.

- Daily bread can pertain to feed me today and tomorrow.
- Daily bread means that I may be mourning in this moment and know joy in the next.

Considerations and Resources

- Consider having various breads represented in the worship service.
- One of the most powerful song lyrics in the African American church is found in the hymn, "Guide Me, O Thou Great Jehovah" by William Williams:

> Bread of heaven,
> bread of heaven,
> feed me till I want no more.

Sing this hymn before, after, or possibly during the message.

• If preaching this message on a Communion Sunday, consider blending the sermon and the observance of the Lord's Supper.

• Biscuits are an African American favorite. Have some prepared for a post-church gathering and sermon discussion.

My Thoughts and Ideas

_____

_____

_____

_____

_____

Battle Lessons

Charles Henry

Text
Joshua 6

Theme
To identify lessons from "The Battle of Jericho" that can be applied to daily living.

Sermon Outline
A MIGHTY EXAMPLE

This is an excellent example of faith! Trusting God to bring down the walls of Jericho seemed foolish. However, God works through foolish ways and means. Israel faced an impossible task. But they served a God who does the impossible.

ISRAEL'S OPTION
- Israel didn't have to follow God's commands.
- God had a plan.

ISRAEL'S OBEDIENCE
- God's time and ways are different.
- God's plan ensures success.

OPTING FOR OBEDIENCE IN LIFE
- We always have a choice.
- Our choices determine our defeats and our successes.
- Obedience is the key to receiving from God. You need not understand all the details, just trust God. Trust God for the

304

impossible. Learn to hear and obey God regardless of how foolish it may seem.

Considerations and Resources

• What are the negative and positive understandings associated with *obey* and *obedience*?

• Listen to the spiritual "Joshua Fought the Battle of Jericho." What sentiments does your listening inspire?

• *Battle* is a term of violence. Do you think it is wise to monitor the use of such terms in preaching? Why or why not?

My Thoughts and Ideas

_____

_____

_____

_____

_____

FIRST SUNDAY OF ADVENT

Beyond a Reasonable Hope

Cedric Kirkland Harris

Text

Romans 4:18*a*

Theme

To explore the cryptic meaning of this text as it meets our experiences of hopelessness and hope.

Sermon Outline

REASONABLE HOPE

In the face of our various situations and circumstances, what can we reasonably hope for? What are our realistic expectations? What are the best-case scenarios?

WHEN A REASONABLE HOPE IS UNREASONABLE

What happens within us and with our families and friends when a reasonable hope or expectation is unreasonable, insufficient, or fails to console our souls? What is our emotional response when a reasonable hope is hopeless? Grief is the primary emotional response. Grief is the emotional cousin, the walking partner, the weeping wet pillow, "the good morning heartache" (Billie Holiday) of hopelessness. Hopelessness opens the door to despair, even a despair regarding a reasonable hope. Hopelessness exposes the crack in our faith armor (Ephesians 6:11). When a reasonable hope or expectation does not meet what we truly desire, we grieve over our loss of life.

To Hope Beyond a Reasonable Hope

• Desperation?—"Against all hope, Abraham in hope believed." Transpose this cryptic scripture: "Against all reasonable hope, Abraham in hope believed in God." Was Abraham's reaction, and is our reaction, to hopelessness as an upward turn to God an act of desperation or a response to an invitation? Perhaps both! There is nothing wrong with turning to God in desperation. More than once and in more than one way, the psalmist, in desperation, cries out to the Lord, and the Lord hears the anguished cry. When we are desperate and have nowhere to go, we can always go to God.

• Invitation—Abraham's call was an invitation from God, but even God's invitation can seem to be an unreasonable hope. The bidding of the Spirit will not always make sense to us. But here we are not talking about the everyday or the mundane. We are not talking about a reasonable or unreasonable hope for a new house in a new neighborhood with a new car or two in the driveway. We are not talking about simply calculating our reasonable hope or miscalculating a hope grounded in our faith in God. No, we are talking about our facing life's desperate moments. Here we are talking about the desperation of death. "Abraham faced the fact that his body was as good as dead . . . and Sarah's womb was also dead" (Romans 4:19 NIV). In times like these, we may not even hear the hopeful invitation, but God hears our desperate cry and answers with an invitation that exceeds all reasonable hope.

• Celebration—Hope is the triumphant celebration over death. Hope is the triumphant celebration over dead-end streets called hopelessness. Hope is the triumphant celebration over a life that has lost its meaning, its value, and its purpose. Hope is the triumphant celebration of faith believing that God has the power to do what God has promised (verse 21). Hope is Easter

Sunday's triumphant celebration over Good Friday. Hope is the triumphant celebration of God raising Jesus from the dead (verse 24). Hope is the triumphant celebration of good-for-nothing dead lives being raised to unexpected heights of achievement. Hope is the triumphant celebration of justice running down like fresh drinking water and righteousness like refreshing streams.

Considerations and Resources

• A reasonable hope may be illustrated with the analogy of a "horizontal hope," whereas a hope grounded in our faith in God may be viewed as a "vertical hope."

• Illustrations should be drawn from real-life human experiences. My most profound experience of the failure of a reasonable hope that resulted in grief was receiving news that I had colon cancer and was told what I could reasonably hope for in terms of a prognosis. Although the prognosis was reasonable and what I could reasonably hope for was reasonable, within a short period of time it was unreasonable. My soul was not consoled. Grief and the thought of the end of my life were too much to bear. And so against this reasonable hope, perhaps even in desperation, by faith I turned to God in search for a hope that transcended what was reasonable.

My Thoughts and Ideas

_____

_____

_____

_____

_____

What's in a Name?

Kirk Byron Jones

Text

Luke 1:59-63

Theme

To highlight the significance of naming for experiencing and interpreting life in more meaningful and magnificent ways.

Sermon Outline

FAMILY TENSIONS: NAMING THE BABY

Holiday season family gatherings are times of great fun and great tension. There might be tension surrounding the new boyfriend or girlfriend or spouse being introduced to the family for the first time. Initial inspections can be tough. Sometimes the tension is around that pair of family members that just don't see eye to eye on much of anything.

In the text, there is a tense moment at a gathering of family and friends. They have gathered to celebrate the birth of Zechariah and Elizabeth's son. The name issue is where the trouble starts. Everybody just knows the baby is going to be named after his daddy, the town priest. After all, Zechariah was a great historical name. Priests, kings, and even prophets had been so named. Moreover, the name certainly suited what had happened. After such a long time, Zechariah and Elizabeth would become parents, and Zechariah means "the Lord has remembered." And of course the name would honor the boy's father. No one was more deserving.

Zechariah was so overcome by it all that he hadn't spoken throughout his wife's pregnancy. What other name could the boy possibly be given? Family members were so sure that among the

309

gifts were towels, spoons, cups, and clothing engraved with the boy's name: Zechariah Jr.

After all this, Elizabeth chooses the name "John." Zechariah agrees.

TO QUIVER WITH LIFE

It has been said that words cause things to quiver with life. The biblical understanding of name is that it is an expression of the essential nature of its bearer.

A SEASON OF NAMES

We are in a season now of wonderful names. What will they mean to you this year?

- Elizabeth: God is a promise.
- John: Jehovah's gift, or God is gracious.
- Jesus: The Greek form of the Hebrew name Joshua, meaning deliverer or savior.
- Immanuel: God is with us.

Considerations and Resources

- Research the meaning of your name.
- This sermon begins with a familiar experience of the holiday season. How can you keep your preaching connected to everyday reality?
- This sermon practices "biblical imagination" when it refers to gifts bearing the name "Zechariah Jr." The intent is to create familiarity and humor. Are these honorable intentions in preaching? Why?

My Thoughts and Ideas

_____

_____

_____

_____

_____

December

DECEMBER

ARTICLES

Advent and Activism

Kirk Byron Jones

During Advent, the time of holy expectancy and anticipation, I grieve that we limit such holiness to seasons and services. Indeed, the earth is *always* the Lord's, and the fullness thereof and all that dwell therein. How can we experience authentic sacredness in the ongoing ebb and flow of everyday life and everyday ministry? One way is to begin to see and celebrate the sacredness of our ministries in ways that we are not accustomed to. For example, after the civil rights march in Selma, Alabama, the late Abraham Heschel, professor at the Jewish Theological Seminary of America, said, "I felt my legs were praying." Heschel's brief but powerful statement points, in particular, to the sacredness of justice-making in society. Highlighting the essential holiness of social ministry—and holy Advent is as good a time as any to do this—can lead to increased and sorely needed socially relevant ministry.

First, seeing the holiness in justice-making can renew waning passions for social mission. Decreasing denominational and ecumenical commitment to social engagement is a significant impediment to contemporary social ministry. How would you describe the level of intensity for social ministry in your own church? How might that level be enhanced by reminding ourselves that social ministry is as holy as Advent or any other "religious season"?

Once during one of my flights of homiletical oratory, words flew out of my mouth that had not been scripted: "The church's work in the community is as holy as Holy Communion." Since that first "intrusion," I have made that statement many times on purpose. Social ministry may matter more if we interpret it as a matter at the heart of God, as holy as anything we can do.

Second, nurturing a deeper appreciation for the sacred dimensions of social ministry may inspire us to a more pervasive social ministry: social ministry throughout ongoing preaching and teaching, worship, service, and fellowship ministries of the church. Often social ministry gets domesticated into the portfolio of a smaller "social concerns" group. Although social concern committees have played and will continue to play a vital role in local congregations, the shadow is that the total church never owns social ministry.

The challenge of the day is *pervasive social ministry*: social ministry that pervades all of church life. We may be more inspired to prioritize social ministry throughout all our ministries as we affirm the essential sacredness of social outreach and activism. It is a sacredness as legitimate as the holiness in the air during Advent.

Finally, interpreting social ministry in sacred terms supplies a critical gauge for properly pacing our work. Holy interpretation breeds holistic application. We are inspired to do God's work in God's way, at a pace that avoids violence to the self and to the institutions socially engaged. Thomas Merton's words have been of immeasurable help to me in practicing balance and peace as I do social ministry: "To allow oneself to be carried away by a multitude of conflicting concerns, to surrender to too many demands, to commit oneself to too many projects, to want to help everyone in everything is to succumb to violence."

Let us avoid limiting heightened spiritual fervor to a season and to the encased, albeit precious, place of the sanctuary. May the inflamed spirituality that characterizes Advent and the impossible possibility it marches us toward inspire enhanced ministry: spiritual activism in season and out.

Works Cited

Abraham Heschel, as quoted in *Moral Grandeur and Spiritual Audacity*, ed. Susana Heschel. (New York: The NoonDay Press, 1996), vii.

Thomas Merton, as quoted by Wayne Muller in *Sabbath* (New York: Bantam Books, 1999), 3.

We Are Rosa Parks

Kirk Byron Jones

Where were you when you heard that Rosa Parks had died? What were you doing? How did you respond to the news? Though I had not spoken her name or thought about her recently, I found myself momentarily numbed by the news of her passing. It was as if something precious beyond comprehension had left our world, had left me. So I stopped what I was doing and just sat. We rush everything these days, including our grieving. Let us resist moving past the death of Rosa Parks too swiftly. In tribute to one where sitting changed a nation, we do well to sit and think.

In her book, *Black Womanist Ethics*, Katie Cannon writes about "unshouted courage," calling it "the quality of steadfastness, akin to fortitude, in the face of formidable oppression" ([Atlanta: Scholars Press, 1988], 144). Rosa Parks personified "unshouted courage" in her unpretentious act of civil disobedience on a Montgomery bus nearly fifty years ago, and in the calm though deliberate manner in which she recalled her act in countless interviews thereafter.

What a stunning contrast to Martin Luther King Jr.'s and Malcolm X's volcanic vocal pronouncements. Rosa Parks reminds us that courage comes in many shapes, sizes, and voices, even a voice just above a whisper. The question is not will you or I be courageous like Rosa Parks or any of the sung and unsung champions of the civil rights movement, but will we be true to our convictions in ways that are true to who we are. Will I listen to and own my unique courageous voice? Will you?

I cannot think of Rosa Parks without recalling some of the most profound words I have read concerning her. In *Let Your Life Speak: Listening for the Voice of Vocation*, Parker Palmer interprets Parks' protest as an action whereby she affirmed personal wholeness: she refused to think free and act oppressed. Palmer ponders:

> Where do people find the courage to live divided no more when they know they will be punished for it? They have come to understand that no punishment anyone might inflict on them could possibly be worse than the punishment they inflict on themselves by conspiring in their own diminishment. ([San Francisco: Jossey-Bass, 2000], 34)

We conspire in our own diminishment each time we act contrary to our most honorable and liberating beliefs. We are Rosa Parks each time we have the heart to reject that which holds us down and to reach for that which urges us on. Rosa Parks did not have a monopoly on living with integrity; we can do so each day in our aspirations, relationships, and decisions.

Early in her writing career, Alice Walker was asked by a leading national magazine to write about growing up in the South. Though Walker was pleased with what she produced, the magazine suggested major revisions. Walker refused. In a showdown meeting, Walker was informed that she didn't understand; the piece would have to be changed or it would not be published. After considering the positive effect such an article would have on her budding career and weighing that against her integrity as a writer, Walker responded, "It's you who do not understand. All I have to do in life is save my soul" (Derrick Bell, *Ethical Ambiton: Living a Life of Meaning and Worth* [New York: Bloomsbury, 2002], 62). Rosa Parks's decision was a matter of soul-saving, her own soul and the soul of a nation.

Now, we must be careful that we do not do with Rosa Parks what we do with many of our heroes. We tend to place laudable figures so high on the pedestal of praise that they become untouchable, out of living range. The lessons of Rosa Parks are much too valuable to be stored away in history books and museums. We need her beacon light witness of personal uniqueness and wholeness nearby to behold and manifest in everyday life. In this way, Rosa Parks will not simply be a wondrous woman of sainted dignity and sacred defiance who lived *once*, but a spirit of freedom, justice, and personal integrity who lives *now* in each of us.

December

DECEMBER

December

SERMON OUTLINES

SECOND SUNDAY OF ADVENT

Hope against Hope

Marsha Brown Woodward

Text

Romans 4:18-21

Theme

To remind people that we have within us the power and ability to hope.

Sermon Outline

WITHOUT HOPE?

What does it mean for hope to be unborn? Can you live without hope? What happens to a dream deferred, was the question raised by the poet Langston Hughes. Create a climate in which the hearers feel the questions and maybe even start to ask, "Have I been in a place where I could not hope?"

Hope against Hope

Abraham, the scripture says, hoped against hope. When both he and Sarah were past the age of parenthood, he still believed that God would fulfill God's promise. Hopeless situations still exist.

"The Days When Hope Unborn Had Died"

The second verse of "Lift Every Voice and Sing" paints the picture of a people living in a situation in which it was hard to hope. In fact, the song indicates that it was impossible, even illogical, to hope.

Abraham Had No Reason to Hope

Using both the Romans passage and the Genesis account, tell the story of Abraham and Sarah. Be creative as you tell the story, highlighting the parts that build a case for them not to hope: already seventy-five and it would be twenty-five years before the promise was fulfilled; the wife past the age when women conceive. Help the congregation see that it didn't make any kind of sense for Abraham to continue to believe God.

WE BUILD ON THEIR SHOULDERS

We are where we are because of the hope of others, and yet there is still a need for hope in our age.

The experience of African Americans in the United States has been that of men and women who hoped against hope. Not having the material things that others had or the opportunities for education or work that others had, still generation after generation believed that it would be better for the next generation.

HOW TO ENDURE BY HEARING A FRESH WORD IN THE BIBLICAL TEXT

Here are verses from Habakkuk that challenge us to hold on to hope:

> For there is still a vision for the appointed time;
>> it speaks of the end, and does not lie.
> If it seems to tarry, wait for it;
>> it will surely come, it will not delay.
>
> (Habakkuk 2:3)

Though the fig tree does not blossom,
    and no fruit is on the vines;
though the produce of the olive fails,
    and the fields yield no food;
though the flock is cut off from the fold,
    and there is no herd in the stalls,
yet I will rejoice in the LORD;
    I will exult in the God of my salvation.
GOD, the Lord, is my strength;
    he makes my feet like the feet of a deer,
    and makes me tread upon the heights.
                    (Habakkuk 3:17-19)

Historically for African Americans, hope has been found through faith. How is this true or not true in the congregation you serve? What supports hope-filled living?

Considerations and Resources

• There is power in hope. Read the stories of individuals such as Nelson Mandela and Fannie Lou Hamer who have believed in difficult situations. Try not to make this so simplistic that the hearers aren't allowed to struggle with the difficulty that comes with choosing to believe God.

• Is God calling the congregation to a higher level of trust? Note that, generally, the hope is for something that will benefit the larger community, not just a single individual.

• Consider times when you have needed to hold on to hope, possibly a time of illness for yourself or close family member, a season of unemployment, financial challenges, and so on. How did you cope? What helped you to walk through the season?

• If you include a children's time, consider an activity that allows the children to think about waiting. Waiting for their birthday, for school to end, or for Christmas would be examples of things that are important in their lives.

• Depending on your congregation, this may be a hard concept to preach. Consider other places where there is still a need for hope: South Africa during the time of apartheid and the sense of hope that was within the people as they yearned for freedom, the people living in countries such as Liberia and Congo who have experienced fighting that has required many to live in refugee camps or go to other nations and live in a season of exile.

• Litany of Hope Holders: Consider a litany of women and men who believed in a vision even when it appeared not to come to pass. Include both familiar and unfamiliar individuals: Sojourner Truth, Ida Wells-Barnett, Charles Hamilton Houston, Vernon Johns, Fannie Lou Hamer, and others. Sometimes using the names of unnamed persons such as the countless unnamed women and men who walked for over a year during the Montgomery Bus Boycott, helps in making the connection that ordinary people are called to have a faithful response.

• Review lyrics to "Lift Every Voice and Sing" by James Weldon Johnson.

My Thoughts and Ideas

_____

_____

_____

_____

_____

Embracing the Unexpected

Portia Wills Lee

Text

Luke 1:26-39

Theme

To promote adventuring with God with greater assurance.

Sermon Outline

MARY'S DIVINE ENCOUNTER

Mary was preparing for her marriage to Joseph when she had an unexpected encounter with the Lord's messenger, Gabriel. The angel tells Mary God's purpose, promise, and plan for her life. God speaks to us when we least expect it. Having God's favor means becoming God's partner by actively participating in the vision. Our response must be of acceptance by praying, preparing, and proceeding in faith.

PRAYING TO GOD: MARY PRAYED A SHORT PRAYER

• Mary prayed a one-sentence prayer: "How will this be?" Our prayers don't always have to be long, just direct.

• If we ask, God will answer or give us the strength to wait for the answer.

PREPARED BY THE HOLY SPIRIT

"The Holy Spirit will come upon you and overshadow you." We need the Holy Spirit.

• The Spirit orders help to direct our paths.

- The Spirit shows us how we are favored.
- The Spirit softens our fears.
- The Spirit reminds us of who we are.
- The Spirit reminds us that Jesus saves us.

PROCEEDING IN FAITH
- Risk the unknown.
- Anticipate God's next move.
- Prepare to be blessed.

Considerations and Resources
- Review the definitions and origins of the following words and reflect on the theological significance of your findings:
  - Astonishment
  - Wonder
  - Adventure
  - Imagination
  - Surprise
- Reflect on the following quote by Anthony DeMello: "It's not that we fear the unknown. You cannot fear something that you do not know. Nobody is afraid of the unknown. What you really fear is the loss of the known" (*Awareness: Conversations with the Master* [Chicago: Loyola Press, 1998], 29).
- Tilden Edwards writes of a "wide-eyed open hope" that frees us to be in touch with whatever God is doing. What are the barriers to such open hope?

My Thoughts and Ideas

_____

_____

_____

_____

_____

Week Two

In Mary's Belly: Hope for the World

Cheryl Kirk-Duggan

Text

Luke 1:46-50

Theme

To affirm divine and human blessing.

Sermon Outline

GOD BLESSES US BY CALLING US TO VARIOUS MINISTRIES

- God knows us because God created us.
- God creates us with particular gifts and sensibilities.
- These gifts suit us for particular ministries.
- We are to be open to our ministry and to rejoice greatly.

WHEN OUR SPIRITS REJOICE IN GOD, GOD IS MINDFUL OF US AND WE ARE BLESSED

- Rejoicing is part of our daily worship.
- Mary rejoiced in amazing circumstances.
- Today in the Middle East and in Africa, women are stoned for Mary's fate.

- Sexuality is a gift, and pregnancy is a state of grace not to be taken lightly.
- In ancient Israel, to be barren was a curse.
- We must not take the gift of children for granted.

WE SIN AGAINST GOD WHEN WE FORGET THAT CHILDREN ARE A BLESSING

- We experience mercy when we fear God. The biblical understanding of fear is not to be afraid, but to respect.
- God blessed Mary with Jesus; God has blessed many mothers with children.
- Do we really care for our children? Do you have hope today?
- Think about your hang-ups because of your relationship with your parents.
- God calls us to be a blessing and to bless all children.

Considerations and Resources

- Nelson Mandela's autobiography *Long Walk to Freedom* (Boston: Little, Brown, 1994) should be on every preacher's shelf. Read it first to be inspired by the extraordinary witness of perseverance and triumph. For this sermon, read Nelson Mandela's account of visiting with his fifteen-year-old daughter Zindzi. He had not seen her since she was three years old (pp. 470-71).
- Visit www.childrensdefense.org. Don't just limit your visit to this sermon, return to this site several times during the month to ensure that your preaching remains informed by issues that relate to children.

My Thoughts and Ideas

_____

_____

_____

_____

_____

The Heart of Hope

Cedric Kirkland Harris

Text

Romans 5:1-5

Theme

To explore the heart of the experience of hope.

Sermon Outline

HOPE IS A PERSPECTIVE ON LIFE

Hope, as a perspective or a viewpoint, is obtained by our intellect's grasp of some proportionate understanding of life. We do not and cannot understand all of the possible conditions needed for all of the possible outcomes in life. So hope is, at best, some partial and yet sufficient grasp of some knowledge that offers us some assurance about our futures.

THE PROBLEM WITH PERSPECTIVES

- How do we know for sure? What is the experience of hope that assures us that we can be sure?
- How do we verify our experience of hope? What experience assures us of the veracity, the truthfulness of our hope?
- How do we know for sure that our hope is real and that we are not merely engaged in wishful thinking? How do we know that we are not constructing hope out of the ruins of our despair, only for our self-constructed house of hope once again to crumble and fall?
- How do we know that indeed we are building our hope on things eternal? How do we know that we will not be disappointed again?

THE INNER EXPERIENCE
CHANGES THE OUTER PERSPECTIVE

Hope is an outer perspective on life that has been changed by an inner experience of God's love. Verses 1-4 share with us the evidence of a hopeful perspective, but it is verse 5 that expresses how one arrives at a hopeful perspective. Indeed, our intellects do apprehend, grasp, and take hold of an experience that assures us of our hope. However, this experience of experiencing hope does not come from the outside of us, but rather it is the inner experience of God's love for us! "And hope does not disappoint us, because God's love has been poured into our hearts through the Holy Spirit that has been given to us" (verse 5).

In the words of Pascal, "The heart has its reasons of which reason knows nothing." The change, the transformation, the conversion from a hopeless perspective to a hopeful perspective comes about through the inner experience of a changed heart. Simply put, hope is born or reborn by our experience of God's love for us. Jesus loves me this I know! I know it because I have felt God's love in my heart. This is how we know. It is God's love for us that assures us. This is why there is such a joyful sound, a rejoicing sound, heard in this text.

• Rejoice in God's Glory (verses 1-2). The glory of God is God's self-revelation. God is revealed to us in love through our faith in Jesus Christ. God's love for us empowers us to face whatever we may have to face. Everything about the future will be all right.

• Rejoice in the Joy. Joy is the evidence of hope reborn (verses 3-4). The improbable possibility of rejoicing in our suffering, finding the courage to persevere, maintaining our human dignity (character), and having and sharing with others a hopeful and joyful perspective is evidence of hope reborn in our hearts.

• Rejoice in the Promise. Our hope, grounded in the experience of God's love poured into our hearts, will not disappoint us! This does not mean that we will not have to go through to get through. It does not mean that bad things will not happen to good people. It does not mean that our condition will change, the prognosis reverse, or the cross be taken away. What it does mean is that this experience of God's love will not disappoint you. To know that God loves me, to know and feel that Jesus loves me, assures me, consoles me, and gives me a *speakable* joy. The old Negro hymn says, "If I don't wake up in the morning, everything will be all right!"

Considerations and Resources

• Explore the notion of faith as "knowledge born of religious love" (Bernard Lonergan, *Method in Theology* [New York: Herder and Herder, 1972], 115).

• Explore the notion of hope as a perspective on life in *Insight: A Study of Human Understanding* by Bernard Lonergan ([New York: Philosophical Library, 1957], 701f).

• Examine the notion of the "heart" as a metaphor for "desire" in *Jesus the Liberator of Desire* by Sebastian Moore (New York: Crossroad, 1989).

• Illustrations should come from our experiencing God's love poured into our hearts. It has been the experiences of God's love for others and me that have changed my perspective and have given me hope.

My Thoughts and Ideas

_____

_____

_____

_____

_____

Week Three

FOURTH SUNDAY OF ADVENT

Sleepwalking through Christmas

Kirk Byron Jones

Text

Isaiah 9:2; Luke 1:78-79

Theme

To awaken keener attentiveness to the glory of the season.

Sermon Outline

A CURIOUS MYSTERY

Sleepwalking is one of those curious mysteries of life. How is it that people can walk around and even perform tasks, all the while in a state of sleep? We are not completely ignorant about this phenomenon. It occurs mostly in children, although only occasionally, and most of them grow out of it. There is evidence that it runs in some families.

A sleepwalking patient once shared a story about a family reunion at Christmastime. He awoke one night to find himself surrounded by all his sleeping relatives gathered in his grandfather's dining room.

WAKE UP TO THE HEART AND SOUL

There is yet another way of sleepwalking that we need to become more aware of and develop a greater resistance to: the practice of sleepwalking through Christmas: the practice of seeming to be awake at Christmas through our apparent activity but actually being asleep to the crucial matters of the heart and soul at Christmas.

We sleepwalk through Christmas when we push through it without pausing to witness the wonderful.

• Isaiah 9:2 is a text of multiple wonders. The first wonder is that oppressed individuals are identified as having been able to walk through their spiritual, social, political, and economic oppression. The second wonder, and the evidence that they are not merely sleepwalking, is that they are walking and consciously seeing—consciously noticing—and being empowered by what they see and notice.

• It is a terrible thing to go through Christmas and not see wonderful things with the eyes of the soul and the heart.

• Our Christmas sleepwalking may come about in another way: by our hurrying through Christmas without having hope awakened inside of us. Hope—personal and sociopolitical—is the great common ground of the Advent scriptures.

Considerations and Resources

• In his classic on racial oppression, *Invisible Man*, Ralph Ellison refers to people who practice racial hate and prejudice as "sleeping ones." Ellison warns us, "There are few things in the world as dangerous as sleepwalkers" (New York: Random House, 2002).

• Write your own description of hope.

My Thoughts and Ideas

Seeing What We Cannot See

Cedric Kirkland Harris

Text

Romans 8:24-25 (NIV)

Theme

To explore hope as dream, vision, imagination, and creativity.

Sermon Outline

THERE IS A CRISIS IN NATURE

Every day we are subjected to the whims of nature. Hurricanes, earthquakes, parched earth, and tsunamis all point to nature out of control; at least out of our control. Paul personifies nature to suggest that nature itself is frustrated by its own crisis. More profound, Paul more than suggests that it is the Creator who has ordained this crisis of chaotic nature, and that the Creator has done so in order that creation will share in our human hope and someday be liberated from its crisis and chaos (verses 18-20).

And so the crisis in nature is linked to the crisis in human nature. Human nature is as chaotic as Mother Nature. Both are frustrated by uneven, unpredictable, and unreasonable natures. Both groan in frustration over tragic catastrophes and tragic lives (verses 22-23). Nature and human nature wait for consummation. Together nature and human nature wait to see what the end shall be. Together nature and human nature wait for the Beloved Community and the Beatific Vision, the New Heaven and the New Earth, the New Creation.

WE CANNOT SEE THE END

We do not understand God's ordained end. We cannot see the ultimate. Nor do we understand God's means that justify the end. What in nature and in human nature is God doing? We do not know the end or understand the In-Between—the time and events between now and then. We do not understand God's means, God's causality, God's day-to-day graceful influence on nature and human nature. We do not see the ultimate end, nor do we see or understand the penultimate, the time In-Between now and some Glorious End.

Paul says that we hope for the Glorious End. We even hope and later will say "we know" that the In-Between is "working for the good of those who love God, who have been called according to God's purpose." Still, we cannot see, we do not understand the End or the In-Between. For hope that is seen is no hope at all. The content of a hope that is understood is not hope.

THE NATURE OF OUR NATURE

It is in our nature to reach for what we do not understand, to seek for what we do not have. It is in our nature to dream up stuff. It is our nature to stretch our imaginations and picture a better world and a better self. It is our nature, in the likeness of the nature of our Creator, to create something out of nothing. It is human nature to fill in the content of our hopes and to envision, to see what we cannot see. Whether or not we have it all together, whether or not we have all of the particulars, the exact location of the twelve pearly gates or whether the streets of gold are fourteen or sixteen caret, whether the crystal fountain is Waterford or Wal-Mart, or whether there shall be 144,000 or a number that no one can number, it doesn't really matter!

What matters is the hope burning and living in our hearts by the love of God. What matters is that we dream even at the risk that our dreams turn into nightmares. What matters is that we have a vision even at the risk of blind ambition. What matters is that we create even at the risk of our creations crashing to the ground. What matters is that we imagine something better than the crisis and chaos of nature and human nature.

But wait a minute!

- Wait for the dream, the vision, the imaginative spark, the creative moment. Wait on God.
- Wait for others to see what you have seen. Share your vision first with those whom you trust and be patient for them to see what you have seen.
- Wait and see what happens.

Considerations and Resources

- Martin Luther King Jr., "I Have a Dream," in *A Testament of Hope* (ed. James Melvin Washington [San Francisco: Harper SanFrancisco, 1991], 217-20.
- Howard Thurman, "Keep Alive the Dream in the Heart," from *The Mood of Christmas* (New York: Harper & Row, 1973).
- Renita J. Weems, *Listening for God: A Minister's Journey Through Silence and Doubt* (New York: Simon & Schuster, 1999).

My Thoughts and Ideas

_____

_____

_____

_____

_____

Week Four

CHRISTMAS SUNDAY

The Benediction of a Joyful Hope

Cedric Kirkland Harris

Text

Romans 15:13

Theme

To communicate the parting blessing from the God of Hope.

Sermon Outline

LEAVING JOYFUL

Shortly after this sermon (hopefully sooner rather than later), you will leave this sanctuary. You will leave this world of the sacred and return to the world of the secular. You will leave behind the sounds of "Amazing Grace" and "Kum Ba Yah" and will tap your foot and shake what God gave you once again to the rhythms of 50 Cent and Lil' Kim. I confess that as a youth I was of a generation that went to church because we had to. Later as a teenager, I went to church because I discovered that it was a great opportunity to see the sisters. Later in my twenties, I stopped going to church, period. I did not have to go. No one could make me go. So I did not go! It's a wonder that God called me to be a preacher and pastor. If going to church was drudgery, leaving church was, and on some occasions even now is, a joy.

God, who knows our hearts, must have a sense of humor as we leave church joyfully.

COMFORT VS. JOY

We should leave church feeling far more joyful than when we came. As a student, I remember preaching a sermon at Andover Newton Theological School's chapel, and at the close of the service one student remarked to me, "I feel worse now than when I came!" Maybe it was a rotten sermon. Or maybe it is the fact that on some occasions the gospel will cause the comfortable to feel a bit uncomfortable, as it should. When we considered putting cushions on the pew at Bank Street Church, one concern raised by a number of people was that the folk would get too comfortable. "They will fall asleep on you," said one stern-faced member. When you leave here, you may or may not feel comfortable, but I trust and pray that you feel joyful! It may require that in the next few minutes you repent from some things in you and about you that ought to make you feel some discomfort, yet your refusal to change is in part because you are comfortable with what ought to make you feel some discomfort.

Now, shortly, if you leave here mad rather than joyful it may be because you have not repented. Nothing has changed. You came here mad. You stayed here mad. And you have decided that you will leave here mad! Until you open up your heart, nothing in you or about you will change.

BENEDICTION OF A JOYFUL HOPE

But if you open up your heart, if you give in to your desire to be loved by God and God's people, if you affirm that you are indeed loveable and take down the walls of fear so that people can love you, if you just try to stop being something that you are not and just be real and really you and not fear that the real you is not worth loving, then I guarantee you that in a few minutes when you leave this church, you will leave joyfully, as you should. You will leave with the "Benediction of a Joyful Hope": "May the God of hope fill you with all joy and peace as you trust in God,

so that you may overflow with hope by the power of the Holy Spirit."
- Fill up to keep up. Receive joy and peace.
- Don't leave church without God! Trust in God.
- Share the overflow. Witness to others about your faith.

Considerations and Resources

- This is a pastoral message. More than anything else the listeners must believe that you, as their pastor, love them. If you don't love your folk, don't preach this kind of sermon. It will backfire on you.
- This sermon is intentionally lighthearted and sprinkled with humor. Humor opens the door for joy. People will receive difficult and challenging words far better with a bit of humor. Relax with this sermon and enjoy it as much as the joy that you are trying to communicate. After all, the Benediction of Hope is for you as well.
- This kind of sermon is dialogical rather than dialectical. There is nothing theologically heavy or deep about it. It is not struggling with the Mystery. It is a pastoral sermon, to be filled with narrative and story. As the pastor/priest, you just want to bless the folk that you love.

My Thoughts and Ideas

_____

_____

_____

_____

Hold onto Your Hope

Teresa Fry Brown

Text

Ezekiel 37:9-14

Theme

Encourage the congregation to persevere during loss of spiritual energy or focus.

Sermon Outline

DEFINITIONS

What do we do between crisis and resolution? How do you define hope?

BUILDING THE CASE

- What takes place prior to and after the rejoining of the bones (looking in particular at chapters 36 and 38)? Why are these bones so important? What referents can be used to signify present-day "bones"?
- What attributes make one a prophet? Why should a prophet be believed?
- What constitutes a vision?
- What are the responsibilities of the people in their own demise?
- What difficulties do God's visionary ministers encounter when preaching an unpopular gospel? Why do some preach a compromised message?

COST

What is the cost of obedience to God or other biblical virtues?

HOPE ACTUALIZED

• Carefully walk through the elements of the promise in verses 11-14, phrase by phrase.

• Graves come in numerous forms, locations, costs, and even restricted covenants.

• The bones had been lying in the desert for years. How long should we anticipate or hope for deliverance?

• How do we recognize hope actualized, prayers answered, promises fulfilled, or needs met?

CONCLUSION

• Offer scriptural examples of hope actualized.

• Share quotations about hope.

• Include hymns or song lyrics about hope, such as, "My Hope Is Built."

Considerations and Resources

• A careful reading of the text following the rejoining of the bones yields a rich description of spiritual activation. Consult a medical dictionary or reputable website for a description of skeletal structures and respiration and breathing disorders.

• Read Cheryl Kirk-Duggan's *The Undivided Soul: Helping Congregations Connect Body and Spirit* (Nashville: Abingdon Press, 2001) for a thorough discussion of faith, health, and spirituality.

• Consider ways to reframe the classic "dry bones" sermons in contemporary crises and contexts, varying the focal character or lessening the reconnection of the bones. See Teresa Fry Brown's *Weary Throats and New Songs: Black Women Proclaiming God's Word* (Nashville: Abingdon Press, 2003) for ways to personify nouns and verbs.

• Consult *Preaching about Crises in the Community* by Samuel Proctor (Philadelphia: Westminster Press, 1988).

My Thoughts and Ideas

_____

_____

_____

_____

_____

Week Five

The Peace Promise

Charles Henry

Text

John 14:27

Theme

To create fresh awareness and gratitude for the peace God gives through Jesus.

Sermon Outline

THE BIBLICAL CONTEXT

When Jesus said, "My peace I give to you," he must have really shocked his listeners. The Jews of the first century knew very little peace. Their history was nothing but struggle. From Genesis to Malachi, from Abraham to the end of the prophets, Israel's history had been without peace. For more than a thousand years, she had battled her enemies: Assyrians, Egyptians, Babylonians. And now she was under the oppression of Rome.

THE PEACE THAT JESUS GIVES

- The peace of sufficient resources
- The peace of a disciplined life
- The peace of a clean heart
- The peace of fellowship with God

HIS PEACE OFFERING MUST BE MET BY OUR PEACE ACCEPTANCE

God's peace is truly ours when we invite God's presence into our lives.

Considerations and Resources

- Do a word study on *peace*. What meanings inspire you the most?
- Note religious songs that highlight peace. One of the most famous is James Cleveland's classic, "Peace Be Still."
- Study Martin Luther King Jr.'s words on "violent tension" and "nonviolent tension" in his "Letter from Birmingham City Jail." How might his distinctions enrich this sermon?
- Contemplate the relationship between inner peace and peace in our world.

My Thoughts and Ideas

_____

_____

_____

_____

_____

The Second Most Powerful Force in the World

Kirk Byron Jones

Text

Genesis 1:1-3

Theme

To celebrate imagination as a supreme spiritual force.

Sermon Outline

FIRST

The most powerful force in the universe is God, and because John tells us that God is love, we can say that love is the most powerful force.

SECOND

What is the second most powerful force in the universe? Some possibilities are: hope, forgiveness, courage, and imagination. You can hear it most clearly in the pause between the end of verse two and the beginning of verse three.

• The substance of the pause in Genesis is imagination. Imagination is defined by Webster as "the power of forming a mental image of something never before wholly perceived in reality."

• Imagination is the second because it is a place inside of us where new ideas and pursuits are welcomed and encouraged and new ideas keep life.

• Imagination is second because through it new worlds are created. What is your God-given gift of imagination stirring up inside of you? What is bubbling up inside just waiting and wanting to break out and live and change you and others? How will you choose to celebrate and activate the second most powerful force in the universe in your life?

Considerations and Resources

• Talk to children about their play life. Observe children at play.

• Remember your experience of imagination during your childhood.

• Read or survey *If You Want to Write: A Book about Art, Independence and Spirit* by Brenda Ueland (2nd ed., St. Paul, Minn.: Graywolf Press, 1987).

• Talk with an artist or musician.

• Converse with friends and congregants on the experience of imagination and creativity in everyday life.

My Thoughts and Ideas

CONTRIBUTORS

Rev. Jeffrey L. Brown (ABC)
Pastor, Union Baptist Church, Cambridge, MA

Dr. Teresa Fry Brown (UMC)
Professor, Candler School of Theology, Emory University
Atlanta, GA

Rev. Gilbert H. Caldwell (UMC)
Retired Pastor
Denver, CO

Rev. Dr. Cedric Kirkland Harris (ABC)
Senior Pastor, Bank Street Baptist Church, Norfolk, VA
Virginia Beach, VA

Rev. Charles Henry (AME Zion)
Retired Pastor
Evansville, Indiana

Rev. Dr. Kirk Byron Jones (ABC) (Editor)
Professor, Andover Newton Theological School
Randolph, MA

Rev. Dr. Cheryl Kirk-Duggan (CME)
Professor, Shaw University Divinity School
Raleigh, NC

Rev. Portia Wills Lee (ABC)
Senior Pastor, Trinity African Baptist Church
Mableton, GA

Rev. Marsha Brown Woodward (Disciples of Christ)
Pastor, Fellowship Church
Professor, Palmer School of Theology
Philadelphia, PA

SCRIPTURE INDEX